Patricia Smith's

DOLL VALUES

Antique to Modern
Series II

Cover: K star R #127 baby, courtesy Ethel Stewart
Photo by Ted Long

COLLECTOR BOOKS
P.O. Box 3009
Paducah, KY 42001

The current values in this book should be used only as a guide. They are not intended to set prices, which vary from one section of the country to another. Auction prices as well as dealer prices vary greatly and are affected by condition as well as demand. Neither the Author nor the Publisher assumes responsibility for any losses that might be incurred as a result of consulting this guide.

Additional copies of this book may be ordered from:

COLLECTOR BOOKS
P.O. Box 3009
Paducah, Kentucky 42001

@ $9.95 Add $1.00 for postage and handling.

Copyright: Bill Schroeder and Patricia Smith, 1980
ISBN: 0-89145-128-5

This book or any part thereof may not be reproduced without the written consent of the Author and Publisher.

Printed by IMAGE GRAPHICS, Paducah, Kentucky

The author wishes to thank all who helped in compiling this volume of values. It is through sharing information and pictures that all of us gain knowledge of our hobby. Each collector who sent us information or photos is acknowledged along with the photograph. All other photo's by Dwight F. Smith.

Photos listed along with pictures of Diane Hoffman were taken by Steve Schweitzberger, and the dolls are sold from the shop: Turn of the Century Antiques 1421 S. Broadway, Denver, Colorado 80210, a joint venture by Diane Hoffman and Michael S.E. Kaplan.

Other Books by Author:
Modern Collector's Dolls, Vol. 1, 2, 3 & 4
Antique Collector's Dolls, Vol. 1 & 2
Shirley Temple Dolls, Vol. 1 & 2
Madame Alexander Collector's Dolls, Vol. 1 & 2
Kestner and Simon & Halbig Dolls
Armand Marseille Dolls
Teen Dolls
The Standard Modern Doll
The Standard Antique Doll
My Family of Dolls Record Book
Patricia Smith's Doll Values
German Babies & Character Children
Oriental Dolls In Color
French Dolls In Color

THE WORLD OF PRICES

I wish it were possible to talk to each and every doll collector in person. I try to write information about pricing, to each of you, in my books . . . but when I go to a show, read ads, see price lists, I am 99% sure you are not reading the forwards, or introductions to the price guides!

One of the basic facts of our hobby is this . . . whatever the ''book price'' is, that is the **beginning** of prices and they go up from there. That seems to be how collectors and dealers use a price guide. It does not seem to matter what condition the doll is in, it goes in an ad, or on a table at the book price THAT IS MEANT FOR MINT dolls. Maybe the price guides should all be for a dirty, played with, non-original, hair cut, fingers gone doll and then the prices COULD go up from there and be fair.

Pricing is not a game, but a difficult job that demands daily attention. It is not an area that has much fun about it, but it is a neccessary part of the entire hobby. If selling, the prices are too low, and if buying the prices are too high. There is no ''winning'' for the compiler of prices, but we do the best we can and that is all any of you ask, so this service to you is worthwhile. BUT, I do wish more people would read what the prices are based on, pay attention to the condition of their merchandise, and price it according to that condition.

Prices are gathered from every conceivable place, be it an Antique shop, newspaper ad, doll or antique show, lists from dealers, or actual purchases. When an ''abnormal'' priced doll appears in one of these areas, I wait 10 days and call, if the doll has sold, then I pay attention to it, if not that price is forgotten. Just because you may see an ad with a $400.00 Barbie does not mean any Barbie (or even **that** one) is worth $400.00. The same holds true at Doll shows, so there sits an Alexander Portrait for $1,000.00 . . . if the dealer takes it home with her, that price doesn't mean a thing. If it sold, then that is another story, for have you ever asked yourself ''Where do prices come from . . . who makes them?'' The answer to that is YOU do! By your ''wanting'' a certain doll, it creates the price that YOU, the traffic, is willing to bear. The desire of the collector to own is as great as the desire of the dealer to sell, it is as simple as that.

A price GUIDE is just that: a guide, so that the collector can see what area the value of the doll is placed in. The collector may pay less, thereby getting a bargain, or pay higher and still be getting a good deal, as the doll may be an exceptional example in some way, as it must be remembered that two dolls from the exact same mold may vary greatly. The difference may be in the bisque, or in the quality of the painting of the artist. Exceptionally fine bisque will be pale with delicate hues of pink, no flaws and the artist painting will be even and also delicate.

Items on any doll that are important, are the materials of which it is made and condition of those materials: excellent bisque, unlined (crazed) composition and unmarked vinyl or plastic. The hair must be original with bisque (or quality replaced wig), composition and hard plastics. Vinyl dolls must have un-cut hair. The clothes should be original (rare in bisque dolls), and if not original, the clothes should at least be in the style and materials of the age of the doll.

Again, it must be said that a Price Guide is a **guide only** and prices are based on the conditon of the doll. If a mint and all original doll is in an original box and is totally unplayed with, then it would be referred to as ''Tissue Mint'', and these are extremely rare, so prices in this book are based on the material of the doll as mint, including hair, plus being clean, well dressed and able to enter into a collection without having to be ''fixed up'' in any way. If the doll has original clothes that are not stained, been washed or are torn, and/or has original box, then the price of that doll would be higher than will be reflected in this book.

THIS BOOK IS DIVIDED BETWEEN ''ANTIQUE'' AND ''MODERN'' BY SECTION, WITH THE ''ANTIQUE'' SECTION FIRST, FOLLOWED BY THE ''MODERN'' SECTION. Although, to be an antique, an item has to be 100 years old, and unless made before 1880, it is not a true antique, we have grouped the dolls with a year breaking point of the 1920's.

CONTENTS

5

REVISED PRICES: VOLUME I

The following prices are updated, and reflect the current market values. The listing is by page, so it will be easy to go through Volume I and jot down the current prices.

Page 17
Gigi, 7½'' 8.00
Majorette, 7½'' .. 3.00
Heindel, 8'' 3.00
Page 18
Donna Doll, 10½'' 20.00
Doll To Dress,
7½'' 2.00
Page 19
Wanda Walker,
17½'' 50.00
Page 20
Dionne Quints: Current prices in this Volume.
Page 21 (Composition)
Madalaine, 14'' ... 150.00
Alice In Wonderland
9'' 125.00
14'' 175.00
18'' .... 175 to 300.00
Bride, 9'' 125.00
15'' 165.00
21'' 225.00
Bridesmaid, 11'' ... 135.00
18'' 165.00
22'' 250.00
Cinderella, 13'' ... 150.00
18'' 250.00
Dr. Defoe, 14'' ... 400.00
Fairy Queen, 15'' .. 250.00
Flora McFlimsey,
16'' 175.00
22'' 225.00
Jane Withers, 13'' . 450.00
18'' 550.00
Kate Greenaway,
14'' 300.00
Little Colonel, 13''. 350.00
Little Women, 9'' . 125.00
15'' 150.00
Margaret O'Brien,
18'' 450.00
McGuffey Ana, 13'' 150.00
25'' 225.00
Princess Elizabeth,
14'' 250.00

24'' 300.00
Scarlett O'Hara,
11'' 225.00
21'' 350.00
Sonja Henie, 15'' .. 175.00
22'' 300.00
Southern Girl, 14''. 125.00
21'' 150.00
Page 22 (Hard Plastics)
Violet/Active Miss,
18'' 135.00
Alice, 18'' 125.00
Annabelle, 15'' ... 115.00
20'' 135.00
Babs Skater, 15'' .. 150.00
21'' 200.00
Ballerina, 16½'' .. 175.00
10½'' 125.00
Binnie Walker, 15'' 95.00
Bride, 17'' 165.00
21'' 200.00
Cinderella (poor),
14'' 250.00
Cynthia, 15'' 450.00
23'' 600.00
Fairy Queen, 18''.. 200.00
Flowergirl, 18'' .. 175.00
Godey Lady, 18''. 300.00
Groom, 18''...... 300.00
Hedy LaMarr, 17''. 250.00
Lady Churchill, 18'' 250.00
Little Men, 15'' ... 500.00
Little Women, 14''. 150.00
Madelain, 17'' 150.00
Maggie, 15'' 95.00
Margot Ballerina,
18'' 175.00
Mary Martin, 14''.. 350.00
McGuffey Ana, 14'' 145.00
Nina Ballerina, 17''. 175.00
Patty Pigtails, 15'' . 145.00
Peter Pan, 15'' 250.00
Polly Pigtails, 17'' . 175.00
Prince Charming,
17'' 400.00
Prince Phillip, 17'' . 350.00
Princess Margaret
Rose, 14'' 200.00

Queen, 18'' 275.00
Renoir, 14'' 300.00
Sir Winston Churchill, 18'' 350.00
Sleeping Beauty,
16½'' 350.00
Snow White, 15''.. 250.00
Story Princess, 15''. 200.00
Wendy, 15'' 250.00
Wendy Ann, 16''.. 125.00
Winnie Walker, 15'' 95.00
Page 23 (Cissy)
Cissy in ballgowns.. 225.00 up
Bride 145.00
Bridesmaid 145.00
Century's of Fashion 350.00
In various street
dresses 135.00
Elaine 250.00
Miss Flora
McFlimsey 250.00
Flowergirl 175.00
Gainsbourgh 250.00
Garden Party...... 250.00
Godey 500.00
Lady Hamilton 350.00
Melanie 300.00
Queen in gold 225.00
in white 275.00
Scarlett O'Hara 400.00
Sitting Pretty, 17'' . 150.00
Page 24 (Portraits)
Agatha, 1967 ..... 450.00
1974, 75, 76 ... 300.00
Bride, 1965 ...... 400.00
1969 .... 300.00
Cornelia, 1972 .... 350.00
1973 .... 325.00
1974 .... 300.00
1975 .... 250.00
1976 .... 175.00
Gainsbourgh, 1968. 350.00
1972 .... 175.00
1973 .... 175.00
Godey, 1967 ..... 400.00
1969 .... 400.00
1970-71 ...... 350.00

Coco Godey,
1966 ....1,000.00 up
oya, 1968 ...... 400.00
nny Lind, 1969 .. 400.00
1970 .... 350.00
dy Hamilton,
1968 .... 375.00
ssy Coco, 1966 .. 1,000.00 up
adame Doll, Coco
1966 ....1,000.00 up
adame Pompadour,
1970 .... 600.00
elanie, 1967 .... 400.00
1969 .... 350.00
1970 .... 300.00
1971 .... 300.00
1974 .... 250.00
elanie, Coco 1966 1,000.00 up
imi, 1971 ...... 350.00
ueen, 1965 ..... 375.00
1968 .... 350.00
enoir, 1965 ..... 350.00
1967, 69 & 70.. 325.00
1971 .... 300.00
1972 .... 300.00
1973 .... 300.00
enoir, Coco, 1966 1,000.00 up
enoir Mother, 1967 325.00
arlett O'Hara,
1965 .... 400.00
1967 .... 350.00
1968 .... 400.00
1969 .... 350.00
1970 .... 300.00
1975-76 ...... 200.00
arlett, Coco, 1966 1,000.00 up
uthern Belle, 1965 500.00
1967 .... 500.00
ge 25 (Cissette)
gatha Portrette,
1968 .... 350.00
llerina, 1957-59 . 125.00
rbary Coast,
1962-63 ...... 850.00 up
ide, 1957 ...... 125.00
idesmaid 200.00
issette:
Various street
clothes 135.00
In ballgowns 200.00
Gift set with wigs 450.00
ainsbourgh Por-
trette,
1957 .... 250.00

Godey Portrette,
1968-69 ...... 300.00
1970 .... 250.00
Irish, 1963 .... 400.00
Jacqueline, 1962... 250.00
Klondike Kate, 1963 850.00 up
Lady Hamilton,
1957 .... 275.00
Margot, 1961 ..... 250.00
Mealanie Portrette,
1970 .... 350.00
Melinda Portrette,
1968 .... 300.00
1969 .... 300.00
Queen, 1957 ..... 250.00
1960 .... 250.00
1963 .... 250.00
1972, 73 & 74.. 250.00
Renoir Portrette,
1968-69 ...... 350.00
1970 .... 350.00
Sleeping Beauty,
1960 .... 250.00
Scarlett O'Hara Por-
trette, 1968-
1973 .... 250.00
Sound of Music,
Large set: Gretl .. 125.00
Small set: Brigitta, 125.00
Leisel 200.00
Louisa 250.00
Southern Belle,
1968-73 ...... 300.00
Tinkerbelle, 1969 .. 225.00
Page 26 (Alexander-
kins) Discontinued
African 225.00
Amish boy & girl ... 300.00
Argentine boy 300.00
Bolivia 250.00
Ecuador 300.00
Eskimo 300.00
Hawaiian 300.00
Greek boy........ 250.00
Indian boy-Hiawatha 350.00
Indian girl-
Pocohantas 350.00
Korea 200.00
Morocco 300.00
Miss U.S.A....... 250.00
Peruvian boy 300.00
Spanish boy 300.00
Vietnam 300.00
Cowboy & Cowgirl . 350.00

English Guard 350.00
McGuffey Ana 300.00
Priscilla.......... 275.00
All bend knee inter-
nationals, except
above 60.00
Alexander-kins
(Wendy-kins)
Dressed in various
out fits,
straight leg,
non-walker,
7½ ''....... 125.00
Straight leg,
walker 125.00
Bend knee walker 100.00
Bend knee, non-
walker 75.00
Add 30-50.00 for
un-usual outfits
like nurse,
riding habit,
etc.
Alice in Wonderland 175.00
American Girl 300.00
Aunt Agatha 225.00
Ballerina, 1953-54 . 100.00
Best Man 300.00
Bride .... 65 to
225.00
Groom 250.00
Cherry Twins 225.00
Cinderella 275.00
Cousin Grace or
Karen 225.00
Page 27 (Sound of
Music)
Large set: Gretl,
Louisa, Marta,
Fredrich, Brigitta,
Liesl ..... (each) 125 to
200.00
Large set: Maria ... 175.00
Complete large set .. 1,200.00
Small set: Marta,
Fredrich, Gretl,
Brigetta, Liesl,
Louisa .... 85 to
250.00
Small set: Maria ... 150.00
Complete small set.. 1,100.00
Page 28 (Babies)
Babsie Baby 95.00
Baby Betty 85.00

7

Baby Genius, Com-
position 75.00
 Hard plastic . . 95.00
 Vinyl 65.00
Baby McGuffey,
compo. 125.00
 Cloth/vinyl 50.00
Baby precious 50.00
Bitsy/Butch, compo. 65.00
 Cloth/vinyl 75.00
Cherub, 12'' 55.00
 26'' 75.00
Christening Baby . . . 55.00
Honeybea 65.00
Little Genius, com-
po. 65.00
Littlest Kitten 95.00
Mary Cassatt Baby. . 85.00
Rosebud 75.00
Slumbermate, com-
po. 95.00
 Cloth/vinyl 85.00
Page 29
Bebe Phenix, Closed
 mouth 24'' 2,000.00
 Open mouth 1,000.00
Page 30
Identified French all-
 bisque, 6'' . . . . . 345 to
 450.00
 8-9'' . . . . 500 to
 625.00
French type, 6'' . . . 125 to
 300.00
 8'' 795.00
Page 31
German swivel heal
 all-bisques: glass
 eyes, 4-6'' . . . . . 185 to
 245.00
 painted eyes,
 4-6'' . . . . 185 to
 210.00
 glass eyes, 8'' . . 325 to
 425.00
One piece body &
 heads: glass eyes,
 4'' 150.00
 6½'' 200.00
 8½'' 325.00
One piece body &
 head with painted
 eyes: 4'' . . . . . . 85 to
 100.00

5½'' . . . . 95 to
 125.00
7½ . . . . 125 to
 175.00
Page 32
Bonn Doll, 7½'' . . 175.00
Page 33
Babies: Jointed at
 necks, 3½-6'' . . 125 to
 450.00
 Characters: 3½'' 85.00
 6'' . . . . 100 to
 150.00
Candy babies:
 2½-4'' 35.00
 5-6'' 55.00
Japan: 3½-5'' . . 15 to
 20.00
Bye-lo, swivel
 head, 7'' 450.00
Marked:
 682/14/Ger-
 many, 6'' 150.00
Page 34
All bisque from
Japan:
Ones of good
 quality, 3½-5'' . 15 to
 65.00
All one
piece/molded on
clothes: 4'' . . . . . 5 to 6.00
Jointed shoulders
 o n l y :
 5-6'' . . . . 15 to
 25.00
 8'' . . . . 25 to
 35.00
Marked: Nip-
 pon/name of
 doll: 4'' . . . . . 25 to
 40.00
 6½'' . . . . 35 to
 45.00
Queue San Baby:
 4½'' . . . . 65 to
 75.00
Child/molded on
 clothes: 4½''
 (legs together) 15.00
Nodders: 3'' . . . . . . 40 to
 50.00
Occupied Japan:
 3½-5'' . . . . 4 to 8.00

7'' . . . . 12 to
 15.00
Page 35
All bisque: Japan,
 4½'' 45.00
All bisque boy,
 3½'' 85.00
Page 36
Grumpy, 4'' 25.00
Marked: 5430/Ger-
 many, 3½'' 65.00
Molded blonde hair,
 5'' 100.00
Didi or Mimi 1,200.00
Little Imp 250.00
Wide a Wake-
 Germany 250.00
Wide a Wake-Japan 95.00
Our Fairy 1,000.00
Baby Bud-Germany . 135.00
Baby Bud-Japan. . . . 65.00
Peterkin, 9'' . . . . . . 250 to
 300.00
Baby Darling, 5'' . . 45 to
 65.00
Queue San (various
 poses), 5'' . . . . . 65 to
 75.00
Googly, painted eyes
 to side, 6'' . . . . . 165 to
 450.00
Googly, glass eyes to
 side, 6'' . . . . 185 to
 500.00
Peek-a-Boo by
 Drayton, 4'' 95.00
Page 37
A.B.G., 13'' 225.00
 19'' 325.00
Composition Bye-lo,
 20'' 145.00
Amberg baby, 20'' . 450.00
Page 38
Betsy McCall, 14'' . 50.00
Love Me Baby, 16'' 30.00
Page 39
Toni, 25'' 100.00
Sweet Sue, 25'' . . . 115.00
Toni, 10'' 35.00
Page 40
Toodles, 24'' 50.00
Tiny Betsy McCall,
 8'' 35.00

8

12

13

Patricia Smith's

DOLL VALUES

Antique to Modern
Series II

18" Morimura Character baby. Bisque socket head with blue sleep eyes, open mouth and two teeth. Five piece baby body. Marks: Z/ (M̄B) /Japan/10. Courtesy Penny Pendlebury. Photo by Chuck Pendlebury. 13" - $170.00, 16" - $185.00, 18" - $205.00, 20" - $225.00, 23" - $265.00.

20" Socket head on five piece bent leg baby body. Painted upper and lower lashes with brown threaded sleep eyes. Open mouth with two upper teeth, felt tongue. Marks: B9/ ◈◈ /Nippon. Courtesy Diane Hoffman. 10½" -$145.00, 15" - $185.00, 20" - $225.00.

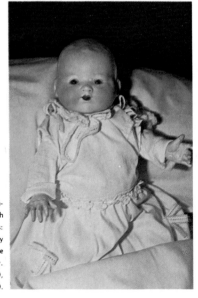

13" long with 9½" head circumfrence. Sleep eyes, cryer in cloth body. Composition hands. Marks: A.M./Germany/351/2. "My Dream Baby" made for Arranbee Doll Co. Courtesy Mary Sweeney. 8" - $165.00, 13" - $265.00, 16" - $325.00, 20" - $425.00.

Large 34'' Kestner on fully jointed composition body. Sleep eyes, open mouth. Marks: J.D.K./ Made in 12 Germany. Courtesy Mary Sweeney. 30'' - $465.00, 34'' - $695.00, 38'' - $800.00.

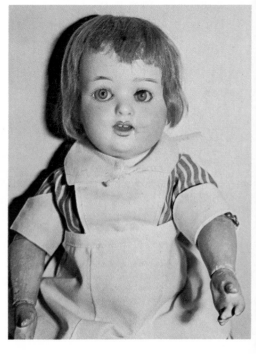

12½'' Bisque head on bent leg baby body. Sleep blue eyes, open mouth wih two teeth. Marks: Heubach-Koppelsdorf/300 8/0/Germany. Courtesy Mary Sweeney. 12'' - $210.00, 16'' -$275.00, 20'' - $325.00, 25'' -$365.00.

18

Skookum Indian dolls. 3½",
6½", 11", 12" & 12".
Celluloid face mask with wool
blankets and wood legs and feet.
Blankets form body that is stuffed
with twigs and grass. Paper labels
identify. Made in USA. Courtesy
Mary Sweeney. 3½" - 25.00,
6½" - $35.00, 11" - $55.00,
12" - $55.00.

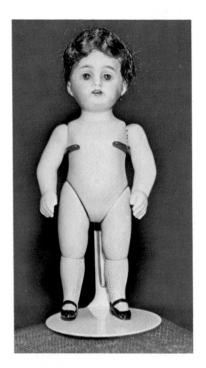

8" All bisque made by Kestner.
Sleep eyes, open mouth with
teeth and painted on shoes and
socks. Courtesy Lilah Beck. 4½"
- $125.00, 8" - $275.00, 12"
-$525.00.

12" Clown with white composition face. Ca. 1924. Original
yellow knit suit with art nouveau
buttons. Courtesy Margaret
Mandel. Unmarked. 12"
-$95.00.

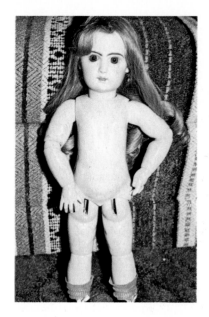

20'' Jumeau showing a typical French body, especially how the knees lack detail and are flush with lower section of legs. Closed mouth. Marks: Depose/Tete Jumeau/8, on head. Bebe Jumeau/Bte S.G.D.G./Depose, on body. Courtesy Mary Sweeney. 20'' - $2,400.00.

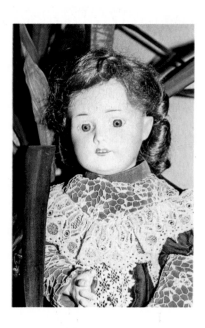

Large 28'' bisque socket head on fully jointed composition body. Sleep eyes and open mouth. Marks: Heubach/250 6½/Koppelsdorf. Courtesy Mary Sweeney. 8'' - $95.00, 14'' - $145.00, 23'' - $235.00, 28'' - $300.00.

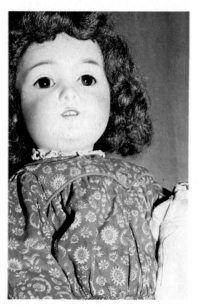

25½'' Bisque socket head on fully jointed composition body. Sleep eyes and open mouth. Marks: Princess/1/Germany. Maker unknown. Courtesy Mary Sweeney. 25½'' - $350.00

2 Unidentified composition dolls. One in trunk is 21'' with painted lower lashes, blue tin sleep eyes, open mouth/2 teeth, eye shadow and bent right arm. Sitting doll is 11'' and has lower painted lashes, blue glassene eyes, rosebud mouth. Both are original. Courtesy Diane Hoffman. 21'' and trunk $75.00, 11'' - $48.00.

13'' Unmarked Twins. All composition and only marked with a 13, on their backs. Blue tin sleep eyes, eye shadow/lashes and painted lower lashes. Open mouth with four teeth. Courtesy Diane Hoffman. 13'' - $55.00 each.

16'' Unmarked twins. Cloth bodies with composition heads and limbs. Cryer box says ''Mama''. Original clothes. Closed mouths, painted upper lashes. Swivel heads on composition shoulder plates, tin eyes. Courtesy Diane Hoffman. $50.00 each.

21

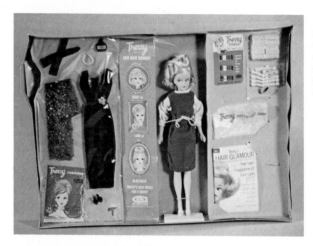

12" Tressy with grow hair feature in original case with extras and clothes. Pale blue painted eyes to the side. Made by American Character. Courtesy Anita Pacey. In case: $25.00, Doll alone: $15.00.

15" Deanne Durbin. Composition with blue sleep eyes, open mouth and human hair wig. Completely original including hairstyle, gown and wig. Marks: Ideal Co. Courtesy Diane Hoffman. 15" -$145.00, 18" - $175.00. 21" -$200.00.

14" Unusual Norah Wellings (England) Eskimo. Painted eyes looking to the side. Courtesy Diane Hoffman. $95.00

Sleep eyes Barbie #1060 and called "Miss Barbie" was in 1964 only. This doll was also the first with bendable knees. She has molded hair with a molded and removable head band, and came with three different styled wigs on a stand. She also came with a lawn swing, planter and the new gold colored wire stand. Her original swimsuit is one piece pink (flair skirt) and she has a pink cap. Head is marked: M.I. The torso: 1958/Mattel Inc./U.S. Patented/U.S. Pat. Pend. $75.00.

8" Ginny in original ski outfit. Wood ski and poles. Felt pants attached to red/white stripe top with suspender trim, matching cap. Straight leg, non walker. Brown sleep eyes, faint lashes above eyes. Blue on white tag: Vogue (only). Courtesy Marjorie Uhl. In outfit: $65.00, Doll nude: $45.00.

2½" Kozmic Kiddle Greenie Meenie by Mattel. Others in series: Purple-Gurple, Yello-Fello & Bluey-Blooper. Solid vinyl with one piece body and limbs. Painted pink hands and feet. Green vinyl head with plastic rolling bead eyes. One green curl and attached pink cap and antennas. Lavneder/pink space ship, which is marked 1968 Mattel. Purple plastic stand marked Kosmic Kiddle by Mattel. Non-removable vinyl clothes. Marks: Hong Kong, lightly on head. Mattel/Inc./Hong Kong, on back. Tag: Mattel Inc./Toymaker/1968 Mattel Inc. Other side: I Glow in the dark, my space ship rolls and I swing around by Mattel. Courtesy Betty Tait. $25.00.

23

16'' Sluggo's Girl Friend. Stuffed vinyl head with molded hair and bow. Head squeeks when pressed. Inset eyes to side. Laytex one piece body and limbs. Cotton dress has white pique collar and sleeves, black bodice and red/green plaid skirt. Marks: S X P/'54. Box information: Copyright 1954 S X P Doll & Toy Co. Brooklyn has comic strip signed by Ernie Bushmiller. Courtesy Elizabeth Mantesano, Yesterday's Children. $85.00.

Unidentified Ice Capade doll using the Kaysam 1961 doll. The Ice Capades did not pay attention to the dolls they dressed, and used any that had an adult figure. They used Madame Alexander, and Italian dolls also. Courtesy Marlowe Cooper. $300.00 up.

24'' Kaysam 1961 doll used for the Ice Capade number "Inca Exotic" 1968. Courtesy Marlowe Cooper. $300.00 up.

Antique and Older Dolls

8'' All bisque with open mouth, sleep eyes and molded on shoes and knee high socks. Most of this type doll will be marked 520 or a number in the 500 series and were made by Kestner of Germany. Courtesy Lilah Beck. 8'' - $325.00.

ALL BISQUE

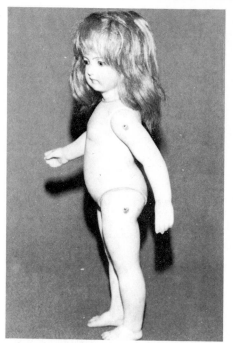

11'' All bisque adolescent fashion doll. Bisque swivel head has set blue eyes, closed mouth and un-pierced ears. The ball head is not smooth but has cranial modelling. Wig is golden-brown mohair. Doll is hip and shoulder peg strung with kid washers lining the five points of articulation. Blush marks on cheeks, breasts, knees and elbows. Fingernails and toenails are molded and tinted pink. Deeply molded eyelids give an unusual downward glancing expression. Rosy lips are outlined in a darker tone with a dark central lip line. Anatomical modelling on base of feet. No marks: Courtesy Magda Byfield. 11'' - $1,200.00.

French all bisques are jointed at the shoulders, hips and necks. They have long slender legs and arms, glass eyes (generally). They can have molded on shoes or bare feet. If originally or nicely dressed, and in excellent condition the following prices are current value: 4½'' Swivel neck, molded shoes - $325.00, 5½'' bare feet - $450.00, Molded shoes - $345.00, 6½'' also jointed at elbows and knees - $795.00.

Shows a closeup of 11'' all bisque. Courtesy Magda Byfield.

ALL BISQUE

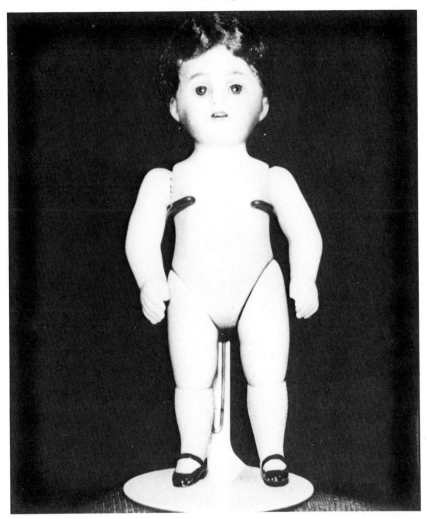

German all bisque jointed at shoulders, hips and neck, with glass eyes, open or closed mouth, nicely dressed or original with good wig: 4'' - $185.00, 5'' -$210.00, 6'' -$245.00, 7-8'' - $325.00, 9-10'' -$425.00.

German All bisque jointed at shoulders and hips only with eyes, open or closed mouth, with good wig and nicely dressed: 4½-5½'' - $150.00, 7'' -$200.00, 8-9'' -$325.00, 10-11'' - $395.00.

ALL BISQUE

9'' All bisque with lovely arms and hands. Sleep eyes and an open/closed mouth. Marks: Germany 156, on back. Jointed at shoulders and hips only. Original clothes, but wig has been replaced with wig of owner's mother's hair. Courtesy Lilah. Because of arms and hands and character face: $395.00.

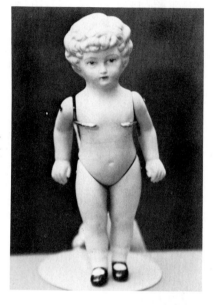

6'' All bisque with modeled hair and painted eyes. Good quality bisque. Pin jointed at shoulders and hips. Marked: Germany. Courtesy Kimport Dolls. $75.00.

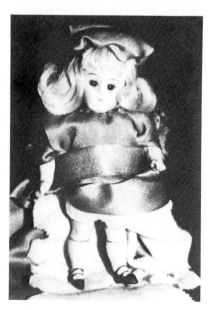

4½'' All bisque with set blue eyes, closed mouth, painted on white socks/blue edge and painted brown shoes. Marks; 620/0, on head and body. 0, on legs and arms. Dressed in old handmade needle and pin holder one piece body and head. Courtesy Mary Sweeney. $150.00.

ALL BISQUE

7" All bisque character child of very good quality. Jointed at shoulder only. Molded hair with painted band, painted eyes and smile mouth. Unmarked. Courtesy Kimport Dolls. $175.00.

4½" German all bisque Campbell Kid with jointed shoulders only. Molded clothes. Courtesy Kimport Dolls. $65.00.

4" All bisque "Tommy Peterkin" of 1915. Molded on longjohns, impish smile and eyes to side (painted). Made in Germany for the Horsman Doll Co. Courtesy Kimport Dolls. $125.00.

4½" All bisque with molded clothes and gun. Marks: Germany, on shoulders. Courtesy Kimport Dolls. $65.00.

ALL BISQUE

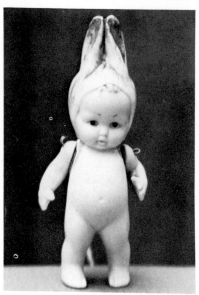

4½'' Heubach Bunny with jointed shoulder. All bisque. Heuback mark on basket in back. Courtesy Kimport Dolls. $95.00.

Shows the side of the Heubach Bunny to show the egg basket. Courtesy Kimport Dolls.

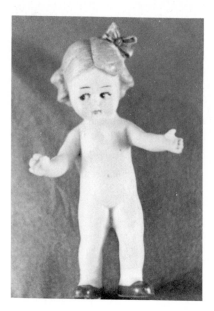

3¼'' All bisque that is molded all in one piece (no moving parts). Molded blonde hair with molded bow, eyes painted to side, and molded on shoes and socks. Marks: 22797-Germany, on bottom of foot. Courtesy Lilah Beck. $40.00.

ALL BISQUE

6½" All bisque Dutch Boy figure. Unusual in this size. Made in Japan. Courtesy Kimport Dolls. $25.00.

3½" All bisque figure molded in one piece. U.S.N., on hat. No marks. Courtesy Kimport Dolls. $40.00.

2" tall Orange Twins all bisque and molded in one piece. Marks: 639/Germany. Courtesy Diane Hoffman. $15.00.

Figurines representing children or comic characters seem to play a part of the doll collecting area so the following prices are listed: 3½-5" - Molded clothes, molded hair and painted features, $15.00 - $25.00. 6½-7½" Molded clothes, molded hair & painted features, $25.00 - $40.00.

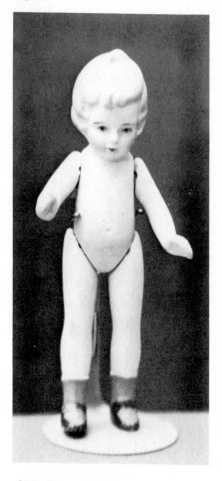

6'' Nodder all bisque boy with molded on clothes and painted features. Jointed neck that lets it "bob". Marks: Made in Japan. Courtesy Kimport Dolls. $30.00.

5½'' All bisque blonde girl. Jointed shoulders and hips. Painted green socks and black shoes. Marked: Occupied Japan. Courtesy Kimport Dolls. $30.00.

"Knotters" called "Nodders" are jointed at neck only and made so that when the head is touched, it "nods". They were made in both Germany and Japan.

German: 4½-5½'' .... $45.00 - $50.00

Japan/Nippon: 4½-5½'' .... $20.00 - $30.00

Comic Characters: Germany: 3½-4½'' .... $45.00 - $55.00

Santa Claus: 6'' $65.00

Animals (Bunny, dog, etc) 3½-5'' .... $20.00 - $35.00

ALL BISQUE

4" Bonnet all bisque with jointed shoulders only, painted eyes to side and painted on orange shoes. No marks. Courtesy Kimport Dolls. $25.00.

5" All bisque that is spray painted. Bow molded in hair. Molded on shoes and sox. Marks; Made in Occupied Japan. Courtesy Florence Black Musich. $15.00.

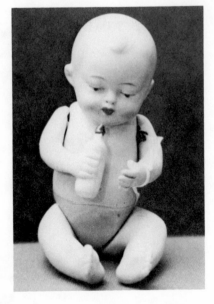

5" All bisque baby, painted on blue diaper and molded bottle in hand. Jointed shoulders and hips. No marks, but most likely made in Japan. Courtesy Kimport Dolls. $40.00.

ALL BISQUE

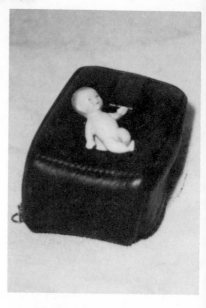

4½'' All bisque. Jointed (re-placed) arms. Painted features. Marks: Germany, on back. Courtesy Penny Pendlebury. Photo by Chuck Pendlebury. $45.00.

2'' long all bisque Bye-lo salt with china glaze finish. (There is a matching Pepper, too). Pink luster finish with blue base. Excellent quality. Courtesy Jackie Barker. $235.00.

10½'' tall all bisque piano baby with molded curls, painted eyes and open/closed smiling mouth. Has eight teeth with red lines between each tooth. Head is turned and is leaning back on one arm. Yellow molded dress with blue bow on shoulder. Excellent quality bisque. No marks. This piece (and others) are and have been reproduced and the purchaser must be alert. For an authentic old piece: $400.00. Suspect of being a re-production: $75.00.

5½'' Piano baby in any position: $85.00 - $100.00

6-8'' with animal: $150.00 - $200.00

6-8'' holding doll/toy/Teddy Bear: $275.00 - $300.00

AMBERG

Louis Amberg began business in 1878 and continued into the 1930's. He had two locations: New York City and Cincinnati, Ohio. He was a major doll importer, but also made dolls and toys. Until 1911 he also had a partner by the name of Ira Hahn.

In 1905 Louis Amberg copyrighted his own work as a doll artist and it was the first known American copyright of a doll's head. The doll was called ''Lucky Bill'' and in 1910 he started using the tradename ''Baby Beautiful Dolls''. Many of the dolls were designed for Louis Amberg by such as Grace C. Wiederseim (Drayton), and Jeno Juszko.

In 1914 Jeno Juszko designed ''New Born Babe'' and the later Bye-Lo Baby (1923) was very much like it. The last doll designed by Juszko for Amberg was in 1915, a portrait of a Zulu, called ''OO-Guk-Luk''.

During 1915 Louis Amberg died and was replaced by his son, Joshua Amberg. This same year Amberg appeared with ''Ambise'' all composition dolls. In 1917 Amberg had Reinhold Beck design ''Fine Baby'', and in 1918, ''Amkid'' shoulder head dolls were put onto the market.

During 1919 and 1920 Amberg used some bisque heads made by Fulper Pottery Co., and these were labeled ''The World Standard''.

In 1921 the Amberg factory burned and dolls were imported from abroad, and by 1924, when Borgfelt advertised the Bye-Lo, Amberg re-issued their ''New Born Babe'' with heads made by Armand Marseille of Germany.

There was an infringment fight, but Amberg lost because he had not compiled with Section 18 of the Copyright Act requiring the full name, and not just the initials of the owner of the doll. Some the New Born Babe doll's heads are marked with an ''R.A.'' and made for Amberg by Recknagel of Alexandrinethal, some were also made by Herman Steiner.

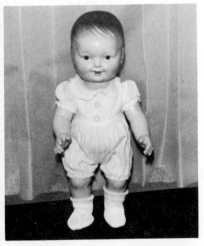

14'' All composition with molded hair and painted brown eyes. Closed smiling mouth. Marks: Amberg & Sons. Courtesy Jeannie Gregg. $95.00

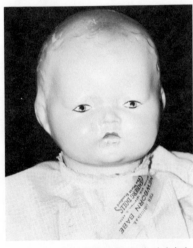

12'' Newborn Babe. Composition head, cloth body and celluloid hands. Pull string makes hands clap together. Tag: The Original/Newborn Babe/Jan. 27, 1914 No. G 45520/Amberg Dolls/The World's Standard. Courtesy Kimport Dolls. $165.00.

ARMAND MARSEILLE

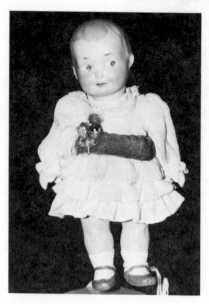

6¼" Googly. Bisque head on mache body with painted on shoes and sox. Intaglio eyes and lightly molded hair. Marks: DRGM/A 11/O M/Germany. Made by Armand Marseille. Courtesy Kimport Dolls. $495.00.

12" bisque socket head with blue sleep eyes. Original human hair wig that is knotted from center of cardboard pate. Five piece, bent leg baby body strung with coil springs. Googly eyes to side and closed smiling mouth. Marks: Germany/258/A O M. Courtesy Magda Byfield. A.M. Googly #253 or 258: 8" $650.00, 12" $1,100.00. #200: 8" $600.00, 12" $995.00. #323 8" $500.00, 12" $750.00. #310 8" $700.00, 12" 1,100.00. #310 Painted Bisque: 8" $275.00.

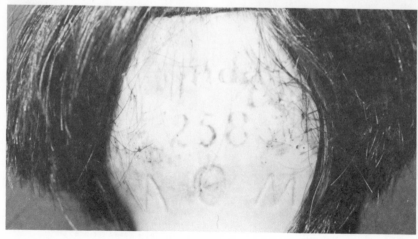

ARMAND MARSEILLE

Mold number 351 has an open mouth and 341 has a closed mouth. "My Dream Baby" made for the Arranbee Doll Co. These babies are called "Rock-a-Bye", but no foundation has been found for this name. 6½" - $150.00, 9" - $165.00, 12" -$250.00, 16" - $235.00, 19" - $425.00, 23" -$485.00, 26" - $550.00.
These babies in Black or Brown bisque:
6½" - $200.00, 9" - $325.00, 12" - $295.00, 16" - $350.00, 19" - $500.00, 23" - $575.00, 26" - $650.00.

12" Armand Marseille's Baby Gloria is shown with 16" Baby Shirley Temple with flirty eyes (marked) and 16" Marked J.D.K. 257 baby. (J.D. Kestner) All courtesy of Gloyra Woods. Baby Gloria: $450.00, Shirley Baby: $225.00 - $300.00, JDK 257: $385.00.

These two closed mouth versions of the "My Dream Baby" are molds number 341 and belong to Gloyra Woods.

13" tall and 9½" head. cir. My Dream Baby made for me Arranbee Doll Co. Sleep eyes, open mouth, cloth jointed body and composition hands. Marks: A.M./Germany/351/2. The name "Rockabye" has been attached to these Dream Babies made by Armand Marseille, and there does not seem to be a basis for this. Courtesy Mary Sweeney.

37

ARMAND MARSEILLE

11½" Armand Marseille dressed all original for the 1894 Columbia. Red/white and blue color clothes. Large set brown eyes, open mouth and on fully jointed composition body with "stick" legs. Marks: 1894/A.M. 6/0 Dep./Made in Germany. Courtesy Kimport Dolls. 11½" - $150.00, 11½" - original $185.00.

22" Bisque socket head on bisque shoulder plate (swivel neck), kid body with bisque lower arms. Open mouth with four upper teeth, and blue sleep eyes. Marks: 1894/A.M. 8/DEP. Courtesy Mary Williams. 22" - $265.00.

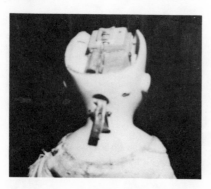

17" Talking Armand Marseille doll. Bisque head with kid body and bisque lower arms. Sleep eyes, open mouth with four teeth. Talk box is in head and fastened with wires bent to fit the grooves in the front and through two holes in the back. The lever for working comes through two other holes in back. Marks: D.R.G.M./201013/A 2/0 M/Made in Germany. Courtesy Jewell Lauren. $300.00.

Front view of D.R.G.M. 201013 Armand Marseille talker with bisque head. Courtesy Jewel Lauren.

ARMAND MARSEILLE

25'' 1910 character baby. Head circumference is 14''
and she is on a very chubby bent leg baby body. Set
brown eyes, open mouth. Marks: Armand Marseille
/Germany/ 990/A 13 M. Courtesy Pixie Porcellato,
New Westminister, Canada. 12'' - $200.00, 16''
-$295.00, 21'' - $365.00, 25-28'' - $500.00-
$650.00.

11'' Bisque head on five piece bent leg baby body.
Sleep eyes and open mouth. Marks: A.M./980/Ger-
many. Made by Armand Marseille. Courtesy Kimport
Dolls. 11'' - $200.00, 16'' - $295.00, 23''
-$425.00.

The mold number ''370'' denotes a head with a shoulder plate, and ''390'' denotes
a head that is a socket head to be used on a composition body.

370 & 390 dolls:

10'' with crude five piece body - $95.00, 10'' on good, fully jointed body - $110.00,
14'' - $135.00, 16'' - $165.00, 18'' - $175.00, 20'' - $195.00, 24'' - $225.00,
26'' - $250.00, 29'' - $350.00, 32'' - $500.00, 36'' - $650.00, 38'' - $795.00,
40'' - $900.00, 42'' - $1,000.00.

Dolls marked with 1890, 1894, 1897, 1914, etc:

12'' - $150.00, 15'' - $185.00, 16'' - $195.00, 20'' - $250.00, 26'' - $300.00,
30'' - 400.00, 36'' - $700.00, 40'' - $1,000.00.

ARMAND MARISEILLE

   Armand Marseille made some very interesting Character dolls, and these are rare, and generally of very good to excellent quality. The following list is of some of these rare mold numbers: May have wigs or molded hair, glass or painted (intaglio) eyes and an open, closed or open/closed mouth:

   400 or 401:

10'' - $500.00, 16'' - $995.00, 18'' - $1,300.00, 21'' - $1,600.00.

   500 - 550:

10'' - $450.00, 14'' - $1000.00, 16'' - $1,200.00, 20'' - $1,500.00.

   560a - Baby, toddler or child:

9½'' - $185.00, 12'' - $250.00, 14'' - $325.00, 16'' - $375.00.

   590:

12'' - $450.00, 15'' - $995.00, 18'' - $1,100.00. 20'' - 1,300.00.

   600:

12'' - $500.00, 15'' - $950.00, 18'' - $1,200.00, 20'' - 1,400.00.

   Fany, Baby or toddler:

14'' - $1,300.00, 18'' - $2,000.00, 20'' - $2,300.00.

   Although the ''Florodora'' dolls do not have a character face, but one considered to be an average ''dolly'' face, the dolls are interesting due to the fact they represent the very famous Florodora Sextette. The 1899-1900 musical comedy ''Florodora (Mis-spelled as ''Floradora'') became the rage of both London and New York, due to the fame of the dainty Florodora Sextette and their song, ''Tell Me Pretty Maiden''. The original members of sextette were: Margaret Walker, Daisy Greene, Marjorie Relyea, Vaughn Texsmith, Marie Wilson and Agnes Wayburn. (Continued on next page.)

ARMAND MARSEILLE
(Florodora - Continued)

The show opened at the Lyric Theatre in London Nov. 11, 1899 and in New York at the Century Theatre on April 5, 1920. The show was revived (different casts) in New York in 1902 and London in 1915 and 1931.

The word "Florodora" was not the name of the heroine, but was an island in the Philipines owned by a wealthy American, who manufactured a perfume also called Florodora (in plot of play.).

Florodora bisque heads came either as a shoulder head or socket head. All are marked with their name with the majority being marked on the head, although some will have a label/stamp on the body and the head marked only with the A.M. (for Armand Marseille).

9-10'' - $135.00, 14'' - $150.00, 16'' - $185.00, 18'' - $200.00, 22'' -$275.00, 25'' -$325.00, 28'' - $395.00, 32'' - $500.00.

15'' Bisque head with open mouth and four teeth. Wood arms and legs with mache body. All original clothes, except shoes. Wig has been replaced, although the original wig was also blonde. Brown sleep eyes. Marks: Made in Germany/390/A./2/ox M. Courtesy of and photo by Clarice Kemper.

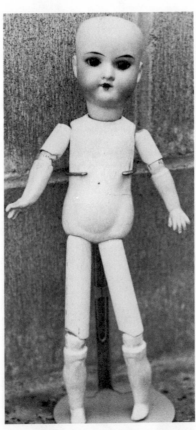

15'' A.M. 390 to show body construction. She has a paper mache body with wooden arms and "stick" legs with very long upper legs. Courtesy of and photo by Clarice Kemper. 15'' - $155.00, 15'' original -$185.00.

ARMAND MARSEILLE

26" Queen Louise. Bisque socket head on fully jointed composition body. Sleep brown eyes and open mouth. Marks: 305/Germany/Queen Louise/10. Made by Armand Marseille and one of the few not marked with their initials or name. Courtesy Mary Sweeney. 10" -$135.00, 14" - $150.00, 16" - $185.00, 18" -$200.00, 20" - $275.00, 24" - $325.00, 28" -$395.00, 32" - $500.00.

9" All original bisque head on five piece composition body. Painted on shoes and hose. Set eyes and open mouth. Marks: 390 A.M., on head. Made by Armand Marseille. Courtesy Kimport Dolls. 9" - $110.00, 9" original - $145.00.

22" Bisque head on fully jointed mache body with wood arms. She is in her original lavender cotton muslin camisole and has original white kid shoes with lavender pom-poms on the toes. Open mouth, light grey sleep eyes/human hair lashes. Marks: Armand Marseille/Germany/390/A 4 M. Courtesy Pixie Porcellato, New Westminister, Canada.

ARMAND MARSEILLE

18'' Armand Marseille doll with talker mechanism in head stands beside the Motschmann type baby. The bisque head is marked: A. 7 M. Courtesy Clarice Kemper. 18'' Baby - $395.00, 18'' - $325.00.

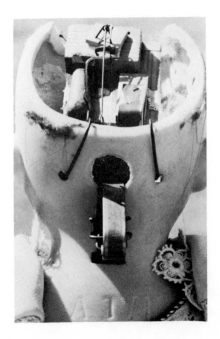

Shows the talker mechanism with control of Armand Marseille doll. Dolls say both Mama and Papa. Courtesy Clarice Kemper.

ARMAND MARSEILLE

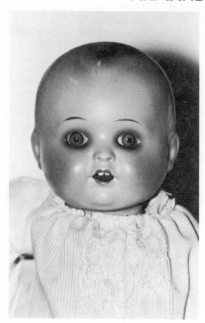

13 ½" Painted bisque baby with set blue eyes, open mouth with two upper teeth and a felt tongue. Cloth body and composition guantlet hands. Marks: Germany/514 8/0. Made by Armand Marseille. $125.00.

17" Painted bisque with five piece paper mache body, blue sleep eyes, open mouth with two top teeth. All original. Mark: A M/2966/0/2/3, on head. Courtesy Nancy Lucas. $145.00.

BED-BOUDOIR DOLLS

Boudoir, or as they are called Bed Dolls, came into being during the 1920's. They are large, but proportioned and of the lady type, and were fashioned after the then popular movie stars. Faces were in the "vamp" style, with some of excellent quality, some fair and some very poor in quality. All were very elaborate, with ruffles of satin and lace, some even having human hair wigs and real eyelashes. The Bed-Boudoir Doll fit right into the Boudoirs of the day, along with the satin spreads and throw pillows.

These dolls were made in U.S.A., France, England, Germany and Italy. Not all Boudoir dolls were expensive, nor even well made. The cheapest had composition heads and shoulderplates made in 2 pieces and either joined or the front half glued to a cloth head. Most all had heavy painted features of the "Vamp", the rest of the dolls were cloth or some had lower arms and legs of composition or celluloid. If there was hair or bonnets, in most cases these were just stapled onto the head.

Of the more expensive Boudoir dolls, they were done more to a classic beauty. Often the faces were painted onto stiffened, shaped cloth like buckrum. Hair is better and the cloth fingers are individually sewn.

The dolls with extremely exaggerated legs, bodies and arms were marketed also as "Flapper" dolls. The Flappers came dressed or undressed and were an imiation of the 1920's Flapper girls, a copy of the movies in caricature. One of the most unique of the Flapper dolls was the "Lindy" (Charles Lindbergh) made by Regal Doll Mfg. Co. in 1929. It has long legs and arms in the typical Bed Doll style, but Regal claimed it to be the "flyer in one of his more jovial moods".

The market for the Flapper, and the good quality Boudoir dolls faded in the 1930's, although a few have been marketed, spottedly, along the years . . . as novelty dolls, with one even being made of vinyl in the 1960's, but the "fad" never caught on again, as it did in the 1920's.

To sum up: the finest quality, well porportioned dolls are called Boudoir dolls. The extra long legged, and armed, rather poor quality dolls are Flapper dolls, and both are rightly referred to as Bed Dolls. (Also see Lenci section of this book for the "Smoker" bed doll.)

32" Cloth with composition head, arms and legs. All original. Painted features. Courtesy Mary Williams. $35.00.

BELTON

No one knows, for sure, who manufactured the "Belton" dolls, nor why they are called "Belton". There was a Widow Belton, and before her just Belton, who made dolls from 1842-46, then went in with Jumeau (or another Belton) from 1865 to 1857. In 1857 F. Pottier was named successor to the Widow Belton's business. There is no foundation to attribute any of the "Belton" dolls to any of these makers.

True "Belton" dolls have a concave area at the top of their heads that are solid (no crown slice) with two holes for stringing, with the wig attached to the holes for stringing, with the wig attached to the stringing material, or three holes with the wig attached by a plug into the third hole.

"Belton" are marked with a number, or nothing. They come on French bodies, both very crude and very fine ones. Many have almost white bisque, with a pink wash blending over the eyes, they can have wide open/closed mouths or lips almost together, but the majority have the area between the lips painted white.

Dome, Bald, Ball heads are different, and most are of German origin. These heads are solid shaped, and completed round without the concave area, although some will have one or two holes for stringing or wigs.

Concave head with two or three holes, excellent quality bisque and body (French) with open/closed mouth. Nicely dressed and wigged: 12'' - $550.00, 15'' - $850.00, 18'' -$950.00, 20'' - $1,100.00, 23'' - $1,300.00, 26'' - $1,600.00.

15'' Flat top "Belton". Doll is strung through the holes into top of head. Some of these dolls have three holes with the extra one to attach the wig. She has pink wash over the eyes, an open/closed mouth and set paperweight eyes. Doll is shown dressed and wigged, as well as undressed. She is on a French body. Courtesy Betty Shelley.

BLACK & BROWN DOLLS

11" Rare Heubach Negro shoulderplate on old cloth body with bisque arms. Has pate slice on top of head that is filled with excelsior. Intaglio eyes and painted hair around head. Marks: 2/0 Sun Mark/Germany. Courtesy Kimport Dolls. 11" - $995.00.

Black, or Brown dolls have become highly collectable and desirable. The most expensive will be the ones with true "Ethenic" features, and not just a White doll painted black.

BLACK & BROWN DOLLS

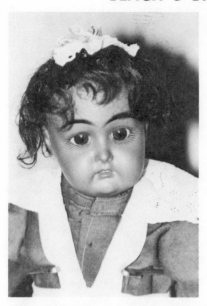

16" German brown fired in color bisque with open mouth and sculptured teeth. Set brown eyes, unpierced ears. Marks: Made in Germany. Courtesy Kimport Dolls. $695.00.

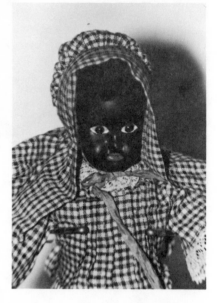

10½" German bisque with black jointed body. Caracul wig, open mouth with four teeth. Ca. 1900. Marks: none. Courtesy Kimport Dolls. $250.00.

12" Brown bisque head on brown fully jointed composition body. Open mouth with sculptured teeth and pierced ears. Probably made by Jumeau. Marks: 3, on head. Courtesy Kimport Dolls. $1,095.00.

BLACK & BROWN DOLLS

11'' Bisque head on composition body, fully jointed and with "stick" legs. Sleep eyes, open mouth. Marks: S, PB, in star H/1909/ 10/0/Germany. Courtesy Kimport Dolls. $375.00.

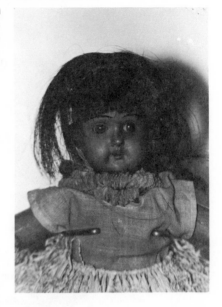

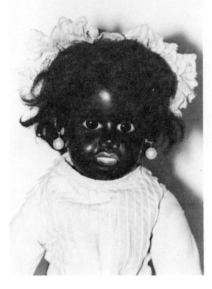

16'' German Negro doll with open/closed mouth, pierced ears and on fully jointed composition German body. Marks: none. Courtesy Kimport Dolls. $775.00

12'' Topsy-Turvy. White and Black heads. All cloth and original. Courtesy Kimport Dolls. $250.00.

18" Tony Sarg's "Mammy Doll", composition head with molded open/closed mouth and painted teeth. Very large composition feet and hands. Cloth body, arms and legs. All original. Tag: Tony Sarge's Mammy Doll/sole distributors/Geo. Borgfelt Corp./New York, N.Y. Courtesy Kimport Dolls. $325.00.

BLACK & BROWN DOLLS

11" Paper mache Negro of 1880 with molded open/closed mouth, and glass inset eyes. Courtesy Kimport Dolls. $250.00.

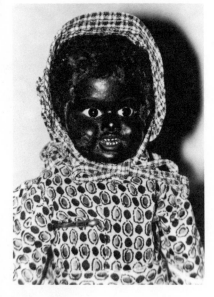

10" German composition on crude five piece body. Painted eyes. Pierced ears and open/closed mouth with two painted upper teeth. Wears grass skirt. Courtesy Kimport Dolls. $125.00.

7" Paper mache of the 1890's in original French Morrocco outfit. Courtesy Kimport Dolls. $110.00.

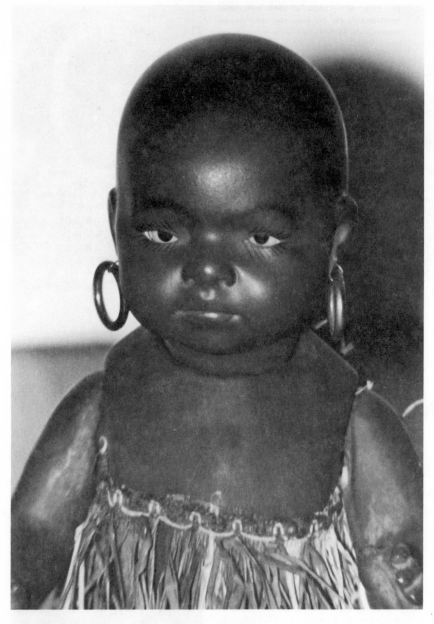

9'' Bisque head on five pieces composition/mache body. Sleep eyes, closed mouth and pierced ears. Marks: Heubach Koppelsdorf/399 13/0 DRGM/Germany. Courtesy Kimport Dolls. $325.00.

BLACK & BROWN DOLLS

10" Black boy with solid dome mache head. Closed mouth, pupil-less black glass eyes and broad features. Wooden body is jointed at shoulders and hips, painted on blue shoes with painted white dots for shoe holes and front slit (where tongue of shoe is), painted long red socks. Head is put on body with heavy wire that runs from holes in neck to his back (below shoulders). Courtesy Pat Sebastian. $265.00.

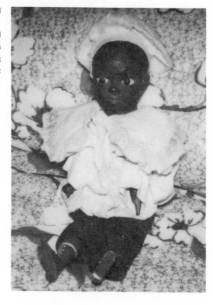

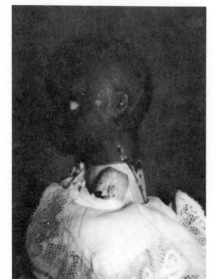

Shows the wire that is looped through the mache head and runs down to the mid-back to be attached to the wood body. (Flange neck).

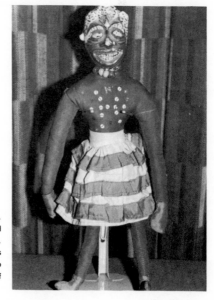

15½" Chocolate brown cotton stuffed head and body. Head with detachable papier mache mask, molded and brightly painted. Red early rayon sewn hands and feet, yellow cotton shirt with red rayon trim. Peking glass bead necklace and earrings, early sequins sewn onto chest. Ca. 1920 from Domey or Haiti. Suggests of voodoo. Courtesy Margaret Mandel. $85.00.

BLACK & BROWN DOLLS

A composition of the Victorian White woman (18'' flat top china), a German bisque scowling Indian with early Indian cradle board, and an 8½'' sitting doll, Indian tanned leather, painted red fringe, Czech., glass beads on German tinted bisque head of fine quality. Painted blue eyes, yellow painted and molded hair. The unusual hood worn by this doll may be a ''capouche'' after the old style worn by Santee for warmth. Head is stitched into garment with no stringing. Ca. 1900-20. Courtesy Margaret Mandel. Standing Indian: 14'' -$250.00, 20'' China - $300.00, 8½'' Sitting -$150.00.

16'' Clay face, hand modelled and painted, one of a kind, not a mold, human hair wig in pigtails. Woodland's Indian beaded blouse under Skookum-type Indian blanket, orange cotton shirt with white polka dots, Skookum-type shoes. Ca. 1920. Very rare to find Indian Beadwork as part of a White Man-made doll. Courtesy Margaret Mandel. $100.00.

15'' Brown celluloid mask doll, painted features, molded over cotton stuffed black head (construction showing at side), human hair wig pigtailed and tied with old pipe cleaners. Straw stuffed body and fully jointed. Commercially tanned leather hands attached with metal strips to arms. Early cotton shirt and fringed pants of cotton, machine sewn. Ca. 1920. Courtesy Margaret Mandel. $95.00.

BONNET/HATTED DOLLS

5 ¼ " Bonnet doll. Bisque all one piece, except arms are wire jointed. Molded on bonnet and dress. Courtesy Kimport Dolls. $175.00.

13" Unusual bonnet doll with intaglio eyes to the side. Cloth body with white bisque lower arms. Courtesy Kimport Dolls. $375.00.

12" Bonnet lady with older look. Molded hat, China glaze finish. Cloth body with white bisque limbs, molded on brown shoes. No sew holes. Courtesy Kimport Dolls. $300.00.

BONNET/HATTED DOLLS

13'' Fancy Bonnet doll. The bands and bows are lavender, cloth body with white bisque lower arms and legs. The head and hat are also of white bisque. Courtesy Kimport Dolls. $325.00.

13½'' Bonnet head of white bisque. Cloth body with white bisque limbs. Courtesy Kimport Dolls. $275.00.

11'' Poke Bonnet white bisque head, gold trim near blonde molded head. Cloth body with white bisque limbs. Courtesy Kimport Dolls. $235.00.

8'' Bonnet doll of white bisque. Cloth body with bisque limbs. Courtesy Kimport Dolls. $200.00.

BRU & CASADORA

Bru dolls will be marked with the name Bru, Bru Jne and sometime with a Circle and dot (⊙), or a half Cirlce Dot (⊙). Bru dolls are found on kid bodies, kid over wood (walking body), or on composition bodies. With the kid bodies, as well as the kid over wood ones, the bisque shoulder plate should be marked Bru, and a number, over the shoulder at the edge.

Closed Mouths

Bru: All kid body with bisque lower arms: 16'' - $4,00.00, 18'' - $4,500.00, 21'' -$4,800.00, 26'' - $5,500.00.

Bru Jne: Kid over wood body, bisque lower arms: 12'' - $5,000.00, 14'' -$5,800.00, 16'' - $6,500.00, 20'' - $7,200.00, 25'' - $7,600.00, 28'' -$8,000.00, 32'' - $8,600.00, 36'' - $9,500.00.

Bru: Socket head on composition body: 14'' - $3,000.00, 17'' - $3,600.00, 22'' -$4,200.00, 25'' - $4,800.00, 28'' - $5,500.00.

Bru: Circle Dot: 16'' - $5,500.00, 19'' - $6,300.00, 23'' - $6,800.00, 26'' -$7,400.00, 28'' - $8,000.00.

Open Mouths

Bru: Socket head on composition bodies: 14'' - $1,900.00, 17'' - $2,700.00, 22'' -$3,200.00, 25'' - $3,800.00, 28'' - $4,200.00, 32'' - $5,000.00.

Composition walker's body, throws kisses: 18'' - $1,900.00, 22'' - $2,400.00, 26'' - $3,000.00.

Nursing Bru (Bebe) Operates by turning key in back of head: 12'' early excellent quality - $3,000.00, 15'' early & excellent bisque - $4,500.00, 18'' early & excellent bisque - $6,000.00, 12'' not as good quality - $1,600.00, 15'' - $2,200.00, 18'' - $3,500.00, 12'' High colored, late S.F.B.J. type - $800.00, 15'' - $1,500.00, 18'' - $2,200.00.

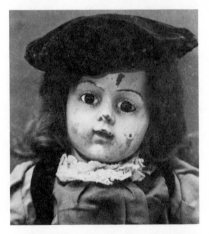

20'' Bru with Gutta Percha head (form of rubber) that is red under the paint. Wood jointed and marked body. Set glass eyes and closed mouth. Head is marked: Bru, this one word only. Courtesy Kimport Dolls. $4,500.00.

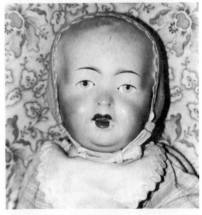

Hand Puppet with bisque head. Open mouth and composition guantlet hands. Cloth covered cardboard holder. Hand slipped in the back to operate the doll. Label says: CASADORA/Original, in circle. Bought on a West Indies Cruise in 1921. Courtesy Kimport Dolls. $295.00.

CELLULOID

3½" All celluloid boy with molded baby bottle. Jointed at neck only. Made in Japan. Courtesy Kimport Dolls. $9.00.

12" Celluloid head on velvet body and limbs, including velvet body and limbs, including velvet "hands" and "feet". This is a copy of the dolls made by Norah Wellings and used as souvenior dolls aboard luxury liners. Marks: Made in Japan. Courtesy Diane Hoffman.

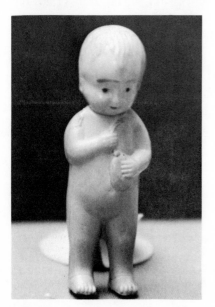

8" All celluloid jointed on at shoulders. Molded on clothes and hair, painted eyes. Marks: Little Orphan Annie on front belt. Harold Gray, on back belt. ☆ /Made in Japan, on upper back. Courtesy Kimport Dolls. $65.00.

CELLULOID
CHALK

17'' Blue painted eyes, straw stuffed Teddy Bear fleecelike body, fully jointed. Shown in 1912 ''Playthings'' Mag. ''in answer to the Teddy Bear Craze''. Doll is unmarked. Head is celluloid. Shown with 17'' Steiff bear ca., 1906, acquired from original owner, fully jointed, straw stuffed long brown mohair, shoe button eyes, long nose, long arms, big feet, hump on back. Courtesy Margart Mandel. Boy - $75.00, Bear - $125.00.

Close up detail of the mask face on the ''Teddy Bear'' body.

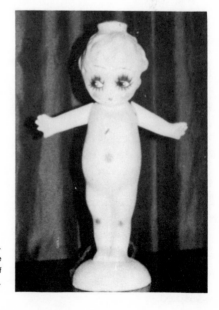

14'' All chalk-like material with jointed shoulders. Molded hair and large painted eyes. This is a lamp base with electric wire from base and light socket in top of head. Marks: none. Courtesy A.P. Miller Collection. $25.00.

CHINA DOLLS

"China" is glazed porcelain, and have been made since about 1740, but did not reach popularity until about the 1840's. The hairdo usually reflects the times of the doll, but not always, as a popular hairdo might have been carried over, long after the same hairdo was no longer in style. A few China heads have the Apollo's knot hairdo of the 1830's, but the most elaborate heads were like the fashions of the 1840's, 1850's and 1860's. One of the "carry over" hairdo's was the "flat top" with curls all around the head as shown in the 1862 London Exhibition, but still made to 1884.

The very early China are rare and therefore very high priced. These early dolls have long necks, adult hairdos, usually a pink "luster" tint, very deep shoulders, the faces generally are thin, and some have the hair split with part in front, and part in back of the ear.

Considered rare in China heads are: Boys, men, head bands, flowers, combs, painted brown eyes, glass eyes, swivel neck, open mouth, pierced ears, bald heads to take wigs and snoods. But, any China should be noted for fine art work and attention to detail, such as brush strokes around the face at the hairline and detail to the eyes and nostrils. Almost all China heads have black hair, but during the 1880's blondes became more popular and by 1900 one out of three of the common type china with wavy hair was a blonde.

Biedermeier or Bald China. Ca. 1840. Has bald head, some with top of head glazed black. Takes wigs. Cloth body, can have china or leather arms: 12'' -$385.00, 16'' -$550.00, 20'' - $800..00.

Bangs full across forehead: Black hair: 12'' - $150.00, 16'' - $250.00, 20'' -$400.00, 26'' - $650.00. Blonde: 12'' - $185.00, 16'' - $285.00, 20'' - $450.00, 26'' - $700.00.

Brush strokes around hairline: 14'' - $250.00, 18'' - $450.00.

Brown eyes:(Painted): 12'' - $450.00, 16'' - $695.00, 20'' - $1,200.00, 25'' -$1,500.00, 28'' -$1,900.00.

Covered Wagon: 1840's to 1870's. Hair parted in middle with flat hair style to sausage curls around head. Many have pink tint: 12'' - $225.00, 16'' - $400.00, 20'' -$595.00.

Exposed ears: Fully exposed, or at least ¾ th exposed: 14'' - $300.00, 18'' -$450.00, 22'' - $550.00, 26'' - $700.00.

Flat Top: 1850's. Black hair parted in middle, smooth on top with short curls around head: 14'' - $140.00, 17'' - $185.00, 20'' - $235.00, 24'' - $300.00.

Glass Eyes came have a variety of hair styles: 14'' - $650.00, 18'' - $1,000.00, 22'' - $1,300.00, 26'' -$1,800.00.

Man or boy: 14'' - $500.00, 16'' - $750.00, 20'' - $900.00.

Pierced ears: Can have a variety of hair styles: 14'' - $350.00, 18'' - $550.00, 22'' - $750.00.

Snood, combs, any applied hair decoration: 14'' - $300.00, 17'' - $495.00, 20'' -$625.00, 25'' -$800.00.

Spill Curls, with, or without head band: Many individual curls across forehead and over shoulders, with all curls ending in points: 14'' - $285.00, 18'' - $500.00, 22'' -$650.00.

CHINA

13" Rare china of the early 1800's. Cloth body with china limbs. Very pale brown hair with flowers on the side of the head. Excellent shoulder detail. Courtesy Kimport Dolls. $1295.00.

23" Unusual hairdo China with black hair. Cloth body with china lower arms. Stipple brush marks on temple and ears exposed. Courtesy Kimport Dolls. $975.00.

15" Rare hairdo china with cloth body and china limbs. Very long feet and white area between lips. Part of ears exposed. Hair is pulled back into very large bun (Braids) in back. Courtesy Kimport Dolls. $950.00.

61

CHINA

20" China with center part. Unique in that she has a molded on blue and white necklace. Cloth body with china arms and feet. Courtesy Kimport Dolls. $475.00.

23" China man with unusual hairdo. Pink luster and smile mouth. Cloth body with china arms. Courtesy Kimport Dolls. $1,195.00.

19½" China of 1875. Full ears are exposed. Unusual hair style and has brush marks curls. Courtesy Kimport Dolls. $450.00.

CHINA

25½" tall China with center part hairdo. Mark: 10, on back of shoulder. Cloth body with attached corset with pink ruffles and bows. Body by Phillip Goldsmith and head made in Germany. Body was patented in 1885. Courtesy Mary Sweeney. $550.00.

24½" China of 1875. Center part with all over curls. Cloth body with leather arms. Courtesy Kimport Dolls. $275.00.

17½" Covered Wagon China. Cloth body with cloth arms and stitched fingers. Large blue painted eyes. Courtesy Kimport Dolls. $425.00.

CHINA

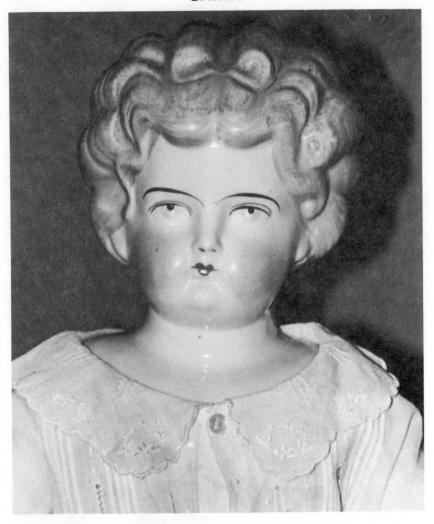

25'' China with dark blonde-almost brown colored molded hair. Large eyes are painted pale blue. Part of ears are exposed. all muslin cloth body and limbs. Two sew holes front and back. Marks: #8, on shoulder. $165.00.

Common hair China, called Low Brow Chinas (Shown above, but with blonde or black hair color) Date from the late 1880's on into the 1900's. Some may be marked Germany, on the back of the shoulder plate: 8'' - $40.00, 12'' - $60.00, 16'' - $90.00, 19'' -$120.00, 23'' - $145.00, 27'' - $185.00.

Pet Name China (have common hairdo) Agnes, Bertha, Daisy, Dorothy, Edith, Esther, Ethel, Florence, Helen, Mabel, Marion, Pauline, and there may be others: 12'' - $85.00, 14'' - $125.00, 17'' - $155.00, 20'' - $175.00, 24'' - $200.00.

CHINA

12½'' Unusual China hairdo, brush strokes on temples. All cloth body. Courtesy Kimport Dolls. $250.00.

19'' China of the 1860's with snood and head band. Cloth body with leather arms. Partly exposed ears. Comb marks through hair and stipple painting brush marks completely around face. Courtesy Kimport Dolls. $600.00.

8'' Tall china head in "Eskimo" plush and fur body. Painted eyes slightly slanted. Courtesy Diane Hoffman. $65.00.

CHINA

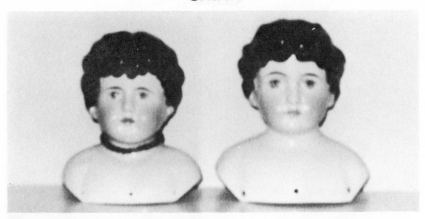

Left: Black hair china 5½'' tall head only: $75.00. Right: Black hair china 6'' tall head only: $85.00. Courtesy Jackie Barker.

Left: Regular bisque head with molded hair and glass eyes. 5'' tall head only: $125.00. Center: 4½'' tall Parian head/painted eyes. Head only: $100.00. Right: Common Blonde china 5'' tall head only: $15.00. Courtesy Jackie Barker.

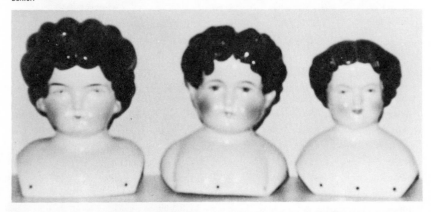

Left: Common black hair china 6'' head only: $15.00. Center: Black hair China 5½'' tall head only: $85.00. Right: Black hair China 4½'' tall head only: $70.00. Courtesy Jackie Barker.

CLOTH

3½" Doll house doll of the 1880's. Needle sculptured and all original. Courtesy Kimport Dolls. $75.00.

6¾" cloth Brownie of 1892. All cloth and lithographed. Designed and copyrighted by Palmer Cox. Courtesy Kimport Dolls. $60.00.

Palmer Cox's Brownies first appeared in St. Nicholas, an illustrated magazine for children in 1883. They were comical, gentle tiny do-gooders who never wanted praise, and must have been a cross (in Cox's mind) between Good Fairy's and imps. The Brownie adventures were known world-wide and filled many children books and magazines. A great many Brownie items came into being and included such things as paper dolls, figurines, cups and spoons, pictures, dishes and rag dolls. The Brownies have brilliant colors, large heads, fat tummies and long, thin elf-like legs. They have long comical mouths. The cloth dolls were printed and home sewn.

CLOTH

17'' Early cloth girl found wrapped in 1923 newspaper. Painted buckrum face, red apple cheeks, brown side glancing eyes, yellow mohair wig, original white organdy dress and hat. Unmarked. Bear is probably Steiff. Ca. 1910. 11'' Fully jointed, long brown mohair with greenish cast, felt pads, hump and glass eyes. Courtesy Margaret Mandel. Doll - $75.00, Bear - $100.00.

8½'' Cut out printed cloth child. Ca. 1915. Straw stuffed lithograph cloth. Courtesy Diane Hoffman.

CLOTH

20'' Barefoot Boy. All cloth with hand painted features, yarn hair. Created and entirely made by Mollye Goldman in 1925 and Registered at a later date. Courtesy Mollye. $90.00.

18'' All felt doll with felt clothes, painted features. Unique in that it has light bulbs for eyes, and has battery pack in back. Eyes light up. Courtesy Diane Hoffman. $35.00.

15'' Felt body jointed at neck, shoulders and hips, four fingers sewn together, painted brown eyes, painted and glazed felt face, brown mohair wig in wig cap, white muslin teddy trimmed in lace, pale blue rayon taffeta dress, lace trimmed, blue felt button shoes. Marks: none. 1938. Original box: Serie A2, Perruque Chala and the trademark (dolls skirt forming A, and Ynal, inside skirt) Bought for owner in 1938. Courtesy Margaret Mandel. $95.00.

69

CLOWNS

10'' Marked Germany jester clown. Bisque head with molded on scarf and painted eyes. Wide open/closed mouth with molded teeth. On new felt body. Courtesy Kimport Dolls. $375.00.

11'' Flange neck clown with glass eyes and smiling open/closed mouth. Original wig. On cloth body with bisque lower arms. Courtesy Kimport Dolls. $475.00.

14'' Bisque head clown with flange neck on mache body. Red wig and glass eyes. Open closed mouth. Marks: 11/0. Courtesy Kimport Dolls. $525.00.

CLOWNS

8 ½'' Bisque head clown with inset eyes, open/closed mouth and a very happy face. Mechanical that sits on a mache cone with rollers on the bottom. Key wind walker. No marks. Courtesy Kimport Dolls. $595.00.

Clown with white composition face. Ca. 1924. Has original yellow knit suit with art nouveau buttons. Brightly painted red lips and cheeks. Unmarked. Courtesy Margaret Mandel. (Also shown in color section). 12'' - $95.00.

12'' German mache squeeze box clown. When body is squeezed he tips his hat and walks. Marks: Germany, stamped on back. Courtesy Kimport Dolls. $165.00.

COMPOSITION
(GERMAN)

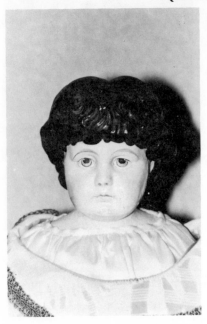

20" Unusual hair style (1880's) Germany composition and very "Kestner" looking. Cloth body with leather arms. Painted blue eyes and black molded hair. Courtesy Kimport Dolls. $350.00.

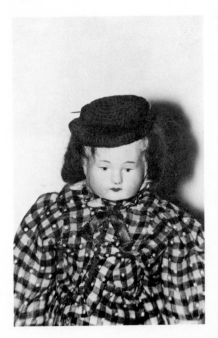

11" German composition of the 1920's. Cloth body with composition lower arms. Courtesy Kimport Dolls. $65.00.

DRESSEL, CUNO & OTTO
DUSERRE, J.

20'' Bisque head with open mouths and sleep eyes on fat toddler bodies. Marks: K star R/126 girl and the boy is marked: Jutta/Baby. The girl was made by the Kammer and Rienhart Co. and the boy by Cuno & Otto Dressel. Both costumed by owner Glorya Woods. 20'' K Star R 126 - $450.00, 20'' Jutta Toddler -$500.00.

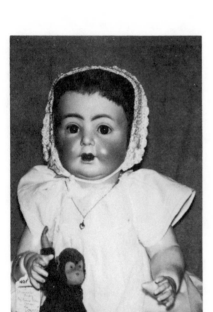

25'' Bisque socket head on five pieces, bent leg baby body. Sleep eyes, tremble tongue in open mouth. Marks: N (script)/62/Jutta/1914/14. Made by Simon & Halbig for Cuno & Otto Dressel. Courtesy Pixie Porcellato, New Westminister, Canada. $650.00.

12'' Late French doll with closed mouth, set blue eyes, unpierced ears and on a French composition, fully jointed body. Marks: Paris/7/J.D. Courtesy Kimport Dolls. This very double chinned, German looking doll was made by J. DuSerre, who made dolls from 1902 to 1908 in Paris. He entered dolls in the St. Louis Exhibition of 1904. $795.00.

EFFANBEE

7" Effanbee all composition doll ca. 1910's. Replaced wig. Has lightly molded on sunsuit and embossed tie and locket. Painted features. Note position of fingers and molded, painted ties on shoes. Courtesy Florence Black Musich. $35.00.

12" Grumpakins (paper tag on wrist). Composition shoulder head on cloth body with cloth legs. Arms are composition. Lightly molded blonde hair, painted blue eyes to the side. Closed, puckered mouth. Original sailor suit. Marks: Effanbee/Dolls Walk Talk Sleep, on shoulder plate. Courtesy A.P. Miller Collection. 12" original/mint - $100.00, 12" not original - $75.00.

20" Bubbles. Cloth body with fat composition limbs and head. Molded blonde hair and sleep eyes. Open laughing mouth with two upper teeth. Not original clothes. Marks: Effanbee Dolls Walk/Talk Sleep, on shoulder plate. Courtesy A.P. Miller Collection. 20" -$85.00, 20" - all original/mint - $125.00.

ELECKRA
FROZEN CHARLOTTE

19'' Very rare Uncle Sam marked: Electra T.N.C.N.Y. White goat's hair wig and beard, painted features, straw stuffed body with composition head and arms. Courtesy Kay Bransky. $350.00.

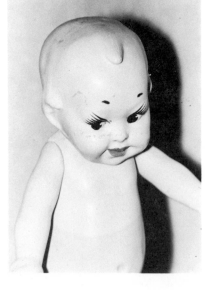

11'' Baby Bud. Souvenir type and made of either paper mache or a composition type material. Painted features, and jointed at shoulders only. Tag on base: Baby Bud by Electra Novelity Co., plus a large red rose. Courtesy Kimport Dolls. $125.00.

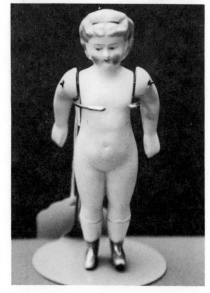

5½'' ''Parian'' Frozen Charlotte with luster lavender boots, pin jointed shoulders and band in hair. She is better quality than a White bisque one. Courtesy Kimport Dolls. $110.00.

FULPER
GOBEL

Fulper Pottery Co. factory was located in Flemington New Jersey and was one of the few American companies who made bisque dolls, so this fact makes the Fulper dolls important. The dolls were made between the years of 1918 and 1921 (time of World War I). The quality of the Fulper heads run from very poor to moderate, by European standards. The Fulper heads were developed for the Horsman Doll Co., but some were also made for other companies, such as Amberg Dolls and the Colonial Dolls Co. Fulper also made all bisque Kewpies in 1920 and an all bisque Peterkin in 1919.

17'' Bisque head on fully jointed composition body. Open mouth with darkly painted lips, set glass eyes. Marks: Fulper, vertically on head. Courtesy Kimport Dolls. $350.00.

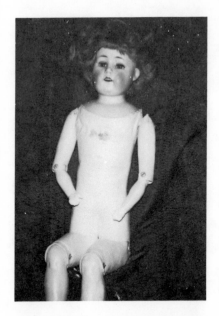

21'' My Daisy made by William Goebel. Registered April 24, 1923 for George Borgfelt and sold through Sears and Roebuck. Bisque shoulder head on white kid body with composition arms and legs, open mouth with four upper teeth and blue sleep eyes. Very long bodied doll. Is in her original box that is dark fawn color with sort of a crocodile pattern. Box contains original straw packing. Marks: . Courtesy Pixie

Porcellato. New Westminster, Canada. $400.00.

H
HALF DOLLS

French dolls marked only with an "H" have not been identified as to maker. A market for them has been created because they are rare, and generally (there are exceptions) they are very beautiful dolls, and very desirable to "advanced" collectors, who may be able to afford them. There are many other exceptional quality dolls that are just as scarce, or even more so, that do not command the prices of the "H" dolls, and no explanation for the difference, except that the market for the "H" was stimulated a few years back, and now it is an accepted "fact" that these dolls should be worth the amount of money they will bring. There is no "rhyme, nor reason" for this, but then, in a number of areas, we doll collectors are not too logical!

5½" Half doll (pin cushion) Marked Germany. Grey curls and one hand molded away from body. Courtesy Kimport Dolls. $225.00.

18" Bisque socket head on composition/wood body with unjointed wrists. Set paperweight eyes, open/closed mouth with tip of tongue showing. Marks: H, on head. Courtesy Kimport Dolls. Head Perfect: $12,000.00, Head Repair: $5,750.00.

4" tall (bust) Half doll-pin cushion. Arms are molded away from body. Marks: Germany. Courtesy Mary Partridge. $45.00.

HALF DOLLS

9" Overall length with arms molded away form the body. An elaborate hairdo. China legs with gold slippers. Marks: 10044. Courtesy Lenora Schweitzberger. Photo by Steve. $65.00.

9" Overall length. Art Deco doll Called "Mimi". Black and white outfit. Wrapped wire body and limbs. No marks. Courtesy Lenora Schweitzberger. Photo by Steve. $85.00.

3" Girl sitting with skirt flaired around her. Marks: 1459 Germany. Courtesy Lenora Scheweitzberger. Photo by Steve. $45.00.

5'' With arms away, but hands molded to doll. Nice quality with unusual look to face. High piled hairdo with feathers. Marks: Germany. Courtesy Lenora Schweitzberger. Photo by Steve. $25.00.

4'' Tall with high hairdo and excellent quality feathers. Arms are molded away from body (one missing). Marks: Germany. Courtesy Lenora Schweitzberger. Photo by Steve. $45.00, Repaired - $20.00.

4'' Has both arms molded away from the body, short, black bobbed hairdo, china legs with gold slipprs. Marks: Germany. Courtesy Lenora Schweitzberger. Photo by Steve. $30.00.

3½'' No open arms of the arms (all molded together) Has lacy blue shawl and is holding a small pink rose. Marks: 16924 Germany. Courtesy Lenora Schweitzberger. Photo by Steve. $20.00.

HALF DOLLS

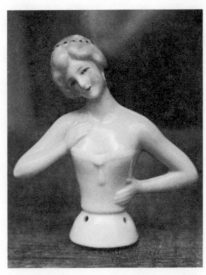

3'' Half doll with arms attached, but molded away from the body. A good quality doll with dotted outline in hair. Courtesy Lenora Schweitzberger. Photo by Steve. $20.00.

4'' doll that forms a lamp for over a bed. Blonde hair, pink tie and rose. Original. No marks. Courtesy Lenora Schweitzberger. Photo by Steve. $35.00.

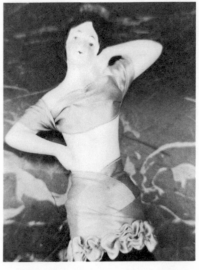

5'' Half Doll brush. All original. Holding dog. Both arms are molded to the body. Marks: 8900. Courtesy Lenora Schweitzberger. Photos by Steve. $18.00.

4'' Black hair with blue comb that has arms attached byspace between. This is an often found doll, but the original wrap is interesting. She is a brush doll. Courtesy Lenora Schweitzberger. Photo by Steve. $10.00.

HEINRICH HANDWERCK

Heinrich Handwerck began making dolls in 1876 in Gotha, near Walterhausen. Thur (Germany). In 1897 Heinrich Handwerck patented a ball jointed doll, and some of these bodies are so marked. As early as 1891 Heinrich Handwerck registered an eight point star as a trademark. He registered such dolls as: Bebe Cosmopolite in 1895, Bebe Reclame in 1898 and Bebe Superior in 1913, although this doll was actually made by Kammer and Reinhart, as they bought the Handwerck factory at the death of Heinrich in 1902 but continued to use the Handwerck trademarks.

17" Bisque shoulder head on kid body that is jointed at the hips, knees and elbows. The body sticker says: Floradora/Germany, but the head is marked: Made in Germany curved around a horseshoe (incised)/W & C 7/0. Made by Heinrich Handwerck for the Welsh & Co. of Germany. Courtesy Mary Sweeney. $225.00.

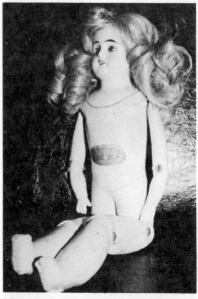

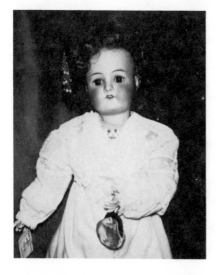

24" Bisque head on fully jointed composition body. Sleep eyes with mohair lashes. Open mouth, with the mouth being very small. Marks: ✳ /1912-4, and she has an incised X, on top of forehead. Courtesy Pixie Porcellato, New Westminster, Canada. $400.00.

30" Large bisque socket head of excellent quality. Paper mache & wood ball jointed body and limbs. Pierced ears, sleep eyes and open mouth. Body is marked Heinrich Handwerck and patented by him in 1897. Marks on head: 109 DEP. 15 Germany/Handwerck-Halbig 6. This head was made by Simon and Halbig for Heinrich Handwerck. Courtesy Pixie Porcellato. New Westminister, Canada. $650.00.

HENDERN, MADAME

"Madame Hendren" was a line of dolls manufactured by the Georgene Averill Manufacturing Co. (U.S.) and the Brophey Doll Co. (Canada). Georgene Averill first began making dolls in 1913 and using the trade name of Madame Hendren by 1915.

14" Doret Doll. Cloth body with composition head and limbs. All original felt clothes. Glued on wig and eyes painted to the side. Closed mouth. Label under right bottom of jacket front: Genuine Madame Hendron Doll, in circle, Doret Doll. Courtesy Marie Ernst. $95.00.

15" Scout. Cloth body with composition shoulder head, arms and legs. Molded blonde hair and painted blue eyes. Impish expression with closed smile mouth. Original clothes. Marks: by Grace Corry, on shoulder plate. Genuine Madame Hendern Doll/Made in USA, stamped on cloth body. Courtesy A.P. Miller collection. $95.00.

HEUBACH KOPPELSDORF

HEUBACH - KOPPELSDORF

15'' shoulder head/kid body: $150.00, 19'' shoulder head/kid body: $200.00, 23'' shoulder head/kid body: $265.00.

15'' compo. body: $145.00, 19'' compo. body: $195.00, 23'' compo body: $245.00.

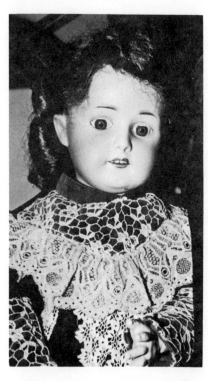

28'' Bisque socket head on fully jointed composition body. Open mouth and sleep eyes. Marks: Heubach/250 6½/Koppelsdorf. Courtesy Mary Sweeney. $300.00.

20'' Bisque shoulder head on kid body with bisque lower arms. Sleep eyes and open mouth. Fur eyebrows. Marks: ✳ /''Celebrate''/1909 Germany/2/0. Courtesy Mary Williams. $250.00.

HEUBACH, GEBRUDER

Marks used by Gebruder Heubach, although many dolls and figurines made by this firm are only marked with a series of numbers: SUNBURST MARK

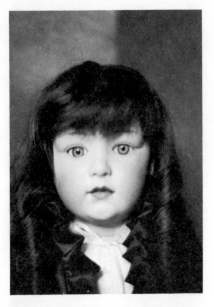

19'' Dolly Dimples by Gebruder Heubach and a very rare doll. She looks very much like the Dolly Dimple made by Hamburger, but the Gebruder Heubach is rarer. Bisque socket head on a fully jointed composition body. Open mouth with dimples, sleep eyes with painted lashes below the eyes. Marks: 717/DEP./"Dolly Dimple"/H/Germany/7 ½/Gebruder SUNBURST MARK. Courtesy Elizabeth Burke. 19'' -$1,350.00, 23'' - $1,500.00.

17'' Bisque character head on fully jointed composition body. Sleep eyes and closed mouth. Marks: 6970/8 (green stamp)/Germany/Heubach SUNBURST MARK. Courtesy Elizabeth Burke. 17'' - $1,500.00, 20'' - $1,700.00.

HEUBACH, GEBRUDER

13" Gebruder Heubach closed mouth pouty with sleep blue eyes. On five piece bent leg baby body. Marks; 72, Heubach in square, 48/4 Germany. . Courtesy Kimport Dolls. $925.00.

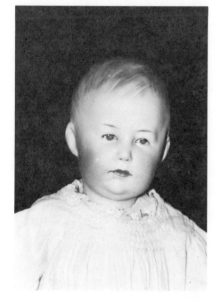

11" Bisque head with intaglio blue eyes, closed mouth and lightly molded, painted hair. He is on a five piece bent leg baby body. Marks: 3/77, Heubach in square 59. Courtesy Kimport Dolls. $525.00.

11" Bisque socket head on composition five piece body with molded, painted shoes and socks. Blue sleep eyes with lashes. Original dress, but replaced wig. Marks: Gebruder Heubach/8-192. Childhood doll of owner Lilah Beck. $300.00

HORSMAN

15½'' Composition head, celluloid eyes, wig is mohair and on fully jointed composition and wood body. The body is a ''toddler''. Made by Horsman Doll Co. and marked: E.I.H/Co., on back. Courtesy Barbara Jean Male. Photo by Michael Male. $495.00.

Shows the back and mark of the Horsman doll, courtesy Barbra Jean Male.

HORSMAN

Grace Gebbie Drayton was born in Philadelphia in 1877 and at age 18 did her first commercial drawing, a cover for the magazine "Truth". Followed by pages in "Booklover's Magazine", "The New York American". It was at this time Grace became wife of Theodore E. Wiederseim, Jr. Many prints and items of advertising are signed with the Wiederseim name. Also during this time the Campbell Soup Company launched a contest for a new advertising idea. Grace Wiederseim submitted a boy and girl holding a can of soup, and these were first used in 1900 ads in Philadelphia's street cars. Their first magazine ad was in the Ladies Home Journal of September, 1905. Grace Drayton went on to a great many illustrations, and in 1910 the E.I. Horsman Company registered the original Campbell Kids. The dolls were made by the Aetna Doll and Toy Company, for Horsman, and licensed by the Joseph Campbell Company. The heads are made of composition patented by Soloman D. Hoffman, a Russian, years earlier (1892). The bodies are cork filled, with attached arms and legs and the very early models just have "mitt" stub hands, where the later ones have composition hands. The very early legs were covered with either red or blue striped material to simulate stockings and the black slippers were sewn to the feet. The latter ones had legs made of the same material as the body, and separate shoes and socks. These early Campbell Kids came in several different sizes.

15" Early Horsman Campbell Kid. The patent for this doll was granted to Horsman on March. 19, 1912. Designer was Grace Drayton. Composition head, hands and legs on tightly stuffed cloth body. Courtesy Esther Gallagher. $95.00.

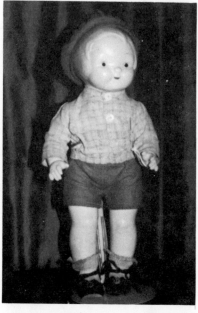

13½" Peterkin. Cloth body with composition head, arms and legs. Molded blonde hair and painted blue eyes. Closed mouth. Original clothes with "Peterkin" tag on hat. Marks: E.I.H. Co. Inc., on back of head. Horsman Doll Mfg. in USA, on tag on shirt. Courtesy A.P. Miller Collection. $110.00.

HORSMAN

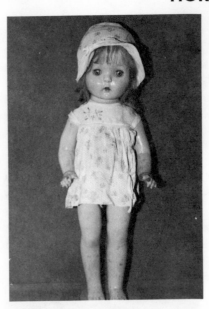

19½" Petite Sally. All composition, tin sleep eyes and all original. Mohair wig. Marked on back of head. Courtesy Florence Black Musich. $85.00.

26" Cloth with composition head and limbs. Cryer in back. Open mouth and celluloid over tin sleep eyes. One of the large, "Mama" Gold Medal dolls of the 1920's. Courtesy Mary Williams. $125.00

10" Sweet Marie of 1915. Composition head on sawdust filled cloth body. The sawdust filled arms and legs are attached with a heavy wire and joined to each other through the body. (Both arms or legs move when one side is moved). Blue painted eyes to the side. "Corkscrew", also called "sausage" curls surround head. Courtesy Mrs. C. Rady. $75.00.

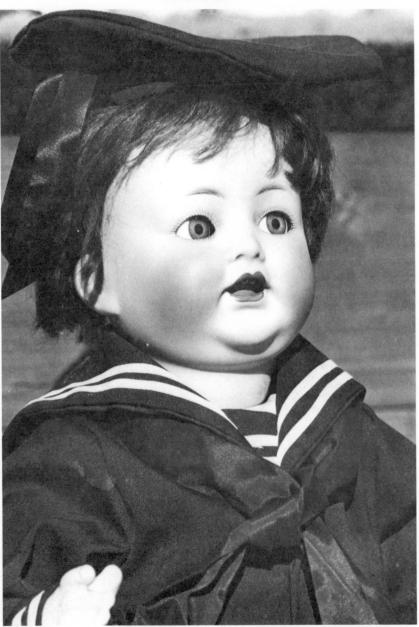

19'' Bisque socket head on five piece, bent leg baby. Open mouth with two teeth. Voice box in body. Blue flirty and sleep eyes. Marks: ✕ /Simon & Halbig/ (AB W) /Made in Germany/1916. Made for A. Hulss. Courtesy of and photo by Clarice Kemper. $350.00.

IDEAL
JUMEAU

Ideal Novelty and Toy Company (Brooklyn, N.Y.) started business in 1907 and founded by Morris Michtom. The first ads by them, to appear in Playthings Magazine, was in 1911 and their dolls included Baby Mine, Dandy Kid and Ty Cobb. The Ideal Novelty and Toy Company is one of the few companies to survive the years, and are still in business.

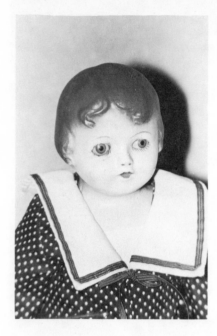

15'' Elsie. 1918. Early glue process composition with molded orange hair, individual rocker sleep tin eyes. Cloth body with rubber hands to just above wrist, cloth legs with molded on rubber boots. Marks: Ideal, in diamond on back of shoulder. Sailor dress may be original. Courtesy Kimport Dolls. $75.00.

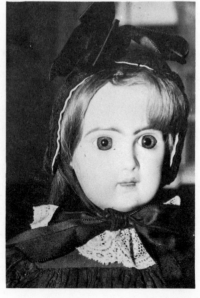

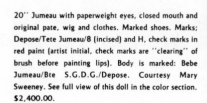

20'' Jumeau with paperweight eyes, closed mouth and original pate, wig and clothes. Marked shoes. Marks; Depose/Tete Jumeau/8 (incised) and H, check marks in red paint (artist initial, check marks are ''clearing'' of brush before painting lips). Body is marked: Bebe Jumeau/Bte S.G.D.G./Depose. Courtesy Mary Sweeney. See full view of this doll in the color section. $2,400.00.

JUMEAU

Tete Jumeau: closed mouth: 10'' - $1,300.00, 14'' - $1,800.00, 16'' - $2,000.00, 19'' - $2,300.00, 21'' - $2,500.00, 23'' - $2,700.00, 25'' - $2,900.00, 28'' -$3,200.00, 30'' - $3,500.00.

Tete Jumeau: open mouth: 10'' - $350.00, 14'' - $500.00, 16'' - $750.00, 19'' -$900.00, 21'' - $1,100.00, 23'' - $1,300.00, 25'' - $1,500.00, 28'' -$1,700.00, 30'' - $1,900.00.

1907 Jumeau: open mouth: 14'' - $500.00, 17'' - $825.00, 20'' - $1,000.00, 25'' -$1,500.00, 28'' - $1,700.00, 32'' - $2,000.00.

E.J. (incised) Jumeau: closed mouth: 10'' - $1,800.00, 14'' - $2,300.00, 16'' -$2,500.00, 19'' - $3,000.00, 21'' - $3,200.00.

Long Face: closed mouth: 21'' - $6,500.00, 25'' - $7,200.00, 30'' - $8,500.00.

Portrait Jumeau: closed mouth: 16'' - $2,000.00, 20'' - $2,600.00.

Phonograph in body Jumeau: open mouth: 20'' - $2,000.00, 25'' - $2,500.00.

200 Series: character (marked) Jumeau's: 19'' - $8,000.00 up.

S.F.B.J. marked, or Unis marked Jumeaus: open mouth: 16'' - $500.00, 20'' -$700.00. Closed mouth: 16'' - $1,100.00, 20'' - $1,300.00.

14½'' Jumeau with paperweight eyes, closed mouth and on fully jointed composition and wood body. Marked: Tete Jumeau, on head. Courtesy Kimport Dolls. $1,895.00.

JUMEAU

20'' Beautiful bisque head with large brown eyes on fully jointed Jumeau body. Head is marked: 192/with a -12- low on neck. Closed mouth. The ''192'' has been identified as a Jumeau doll by other authors. Courtesy Jan Cook. $2,300.00.

25'' Jumeau that is marked: 1907. Open mouth and on a French fully jointed composition body. Shown with her is a 22'' E.D. (E. Denamur 1857-1898) and a Teddy Bear made by ''Alpha'' in England. All courtesy Millie Chappelle. 25'' 1907 - $1,500.00, 22'' E.D. -$995.00.

JUMEAU

32" Very large bisque head on jointed composition body with straight wrists. Open mouth Jumeau, marked 14, on head. Courtesy Glorya Woods. $2,200.00.

20" Late Jumeau with bisque head on fully jointed composition body. Set blue eyes, pierced ears and open mouth. Marks: DEP., on head. Courtesy Kimport Dolls. $695.00.

KAMMER & REINHARDT

Kammer and Reinhardt mold numbers: Characters.

101, boy or girl: 9'' - $850.00, 12'' - $1,200.00, 16'' - $1,400.00, 20'' -$1,800.00.

115 or 115a closed mouth only: 15'' - $1400.00, 18'' - $1,650.00, 22'' -$2,000.00.

115 or 115a open mouth: 15'' - $395.00, 18'' - $595.00, 22'' - $795.00.

116 or 116a closed mouth only: 15'' - $1,300.00, 18'' - $1,550.00, 22'' -$1,900.00.

116 or 116a open mouth: 15'' - $395.00, 18'' - $595.00, 22'' - $795.00.

117 or 117a closed mouth: 18'' - $2,000.00, 24'' - $2,900.00, 30'' - $3,500.00.

Rare #109, 112, 114: 15'' - $2,500.00, 18'' - $3,800.00.

If any of the above mold numbers 101, 109, 112, 114 have glass eyes add: $300.00.

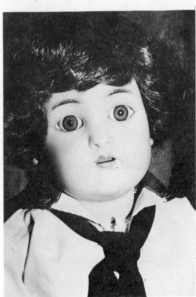

28'' Bisque socket head on fully jointed composition body. Pierced ears and sleep eyes. Open mouth. Marks: Simon & Halbig/K Star R/70, and she has a scroll "W" on forehead. Courtesy Mary Sweeney. $425.00.

15'' Bisque heads marked: K star R/122. (Krammer Rienhart) Open mouth with molded tongue, cheek dimples and sleep eyes. Both costumed by owner Glorya Woods. $350.00.

94

KAMMER & REINHARDT

19½'' Rare pouty marked K star R 114. Sleep eyes and closed mouth. On fully jointed composition body. Original outfit with replaced bonnet and wig. Courtesy Kimport Dolls. 19½'' Perfect - $4,000.00, 19½'' Minor mend to head - $2,250.00.

KAMMER & REINHARDT

25" Bisque socket head on five piece bent leg baby body, open mouth and sleep eyes. Childhood doll of Rose Treanor Markwith and was used as a display manakin at the Wanamaker's, downtown New York City, and was purchased in 1908. Marks Simon Halbig/K star R. Courtesy Stephanie Dolci and Florence Black Musich. $500.00.

10½" Bisque head baby on five piece bent leg baby body of composition. Open mouth and sleep eyes. Two upper teeth. Marks: K star R/Simon Halbig/121. Courtesy Kimport Dolls. $325.00.

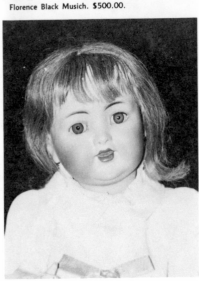

Shows a grouping of Kammer and Reinhart babies and toddlers, all with flirty eyes, marked with the mold number 126. They range from 17" to 23" in size. All courtesy Pixie Porcellato, New Westminster, Canada.

16" Bisque head on five piece composition body. Sleep eyes, open mouth with two upper teeth. Marks: K star R/Simon Halbig/126. Courtesy Kimport Dolls.

KESTNER

16'' Original box with doll and interchangable heads. Made by Kestner. Head on doll is marked: 184, others top to bottom: 178, 174 and 185. All but center one on right side have closed mouths. Courtesy Kimport Dolls. $3,000.00

16'' Bisque shoulder head on kid body with bisque lower arms. Closed mouth, up tilted head and glass eyes. Marks: 172. Made by Kestner. Courtesy Kimport Dolls. 10'' - $1,100.00, 16'' - $2,500.00, 18'' - $2,800.00.

KESTNER

10" Googly with bisque head and large glass eyes to the side. Closed "watermelon" mouth. Fully jointed composition body. Marks: J.D.K./221. Costumed by owner Gloyra Woods. $3,200.00.
Bisque head GOOGLIES: #163, 168, 173, 221, etc: 9" - $2,800.00, 12" - $3,800.00, 15" -$4,250.00, 17" - $4,800.00, 20" - $5,500.00.

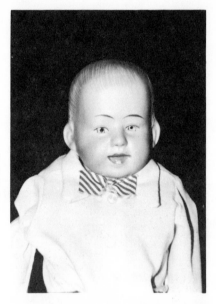

13½" Kestner boy. Ca. 1912. Shoulder head on kid body with bisque lower arms. Intaglio eyes, brush stroke hair and wide open/closed mouth with two lower teeth. Marks: Made in Germany/Ges. No. 216 Gesch./15/0. Courtesy Kimport Dolls. $395.00.

23" Kestner, all original Gibson girl bride. Marks: H Made in Germany 12/162. Original upswept wig and beautiful gown, also original kid gloves. Slim waisted lady body stamped: Germany. Also has label "Made for G.A. Schwarz-Philidelphia-Made in Germany. Open mouth and sleep eyes. Courtesy Emily Liccardi. 18" -$550.00, 23" - $700.00.

KESTNER

Closed mouths, marked with any number, good bisque heads, well dressed, good clean body (Compo. or kid): 15'' - $695.00, 18'' - $795.00, 22'' - $895.00, 26'' -$1,000.00.

Closed mouths, turned shoulder heads: (Mold numbers 169, 639, 969, etc.) 15'' -$495.00, 18'' -$595.00, 24'' - $795.00.

Open mouths, turned heads: 15'' - $250.00, 18'' -$375.00, 24'' - $495.00.

22'' Bisque swivel head on bisque shoulder plate. Open mouth, Blue sleep eyes, unpierced ears. Kid body with bisque lower arms with excellent hand detail. Marks: H Made in 12/Germany/129. Courtesy Kimport Dolls. $425.00.

14½'' Slightly turned shoulder head with closed mouth, glass set eyes and on kid body with bisque lower arms. Marks: 639. Made by Kestner. Courtesy Kimport Dolls. $495.00.

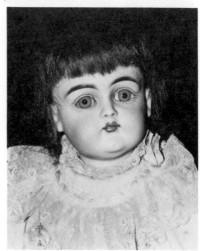

14½'' Bisque head Kestner with closed mouth and sleep eyes. Human hair wig, unpierced ears. All original Marks: E Made in 9/Germany/128. Courtesy Kimport Dolls. $695.00.

99

KESTNER

Children, young adults: Open mouths, sleep or set eyes, jointed or kid bodies, dressed and clean; fur eyebrows: 129, 143, 145, 147, 148, 162, 164, 166, 167, 168, 192, 195, 196, 215, 264, etc: 14'' - $200.00, 17'' - $295.00, 20'' - $350.00, 26'' -$500.00, 30'' - $600.00, 36'' - $800.00, 40'' - $1,110.00.

Any of above 9'' - 12'' in trunks with wardrobe: $700.00.

Most often found mold numbers are: 154, 171, 174: 15'' - $200.00, 18'' - $250.00, 22'' - $365.00, 27'' - $450.00.

In trunks/wardrobes: (9'' - 12''): $500.00.

19½'' Bisque shoulder head with open mouth and sleep brown glass eyes. Kid body with bisque lower arms. Marks: Germany D. Made by Kestner. Courtesy Kimport Dolls. $350.00.

34'' Bisque socket head on fully jointed composition body. Open mouth and sleep blue eyes. Marks: Made in/N Germany 17/146. Courtesy Mary Sweeney. $700.00.

KESTNER

The Ladies Home Journal printed a series of paper dolls created by Sheila Young called "Lettie Lane" and in 1911 "Lettie Lane" introduced her doll "Daisy". (Real doll) The only way to get a doll was to sell three subscriptions, at least one renewal and two new ones, plus $4.50. The promotion included doll and patterns that followed the paper dolls.

The first order for the dolls was 5,000, but they were soon sold out and two factories had to operate for another total of 26,000 dolls before the close of the offer in January of 1912. The "Lettie Lane" paper doll's "real live doll" "Daisy" was a Kestner 174 and also used was the Kestner mold number 171. As you can see with 31,000 given out in the U.S. over a period of only 9 months, and as late as 1911, that is why the mold numbers 171 and 174 are referred to as the Kestner "common mold" numbers.

26" Excellent quality bisque head on fully jointed composition body. Large brown sleep eyes, open mouth and original mohair wig. Marks: K made in Germany 14/171/5. Courtesy Pixie Porcellato, New Westminister, Canada.

KESTNER

Babies or Toddlers: Molded or wigs, good body, open mouths (unless noted) sleep or set eyes, nicely dressed: 121, 132, 142, 150, 151: 12'' - $265.00, 16'' - $325.00, 18'' - $450.00, 24'' - $650.00.
152, 211: 12'' - $275.00, 16'' - $375.00, 18'' - $465.00, 24'' - $700.00.
226, 227, 260: 12'' - $275.00, 16'' - $375.00, 18'' - $465.00, 24'' - $700.00.
Hilda (1070): 12'' - $1,300.00, 16'' - $1,700.00, 18'' - $2,000.00, 24'' -$2,800.00.

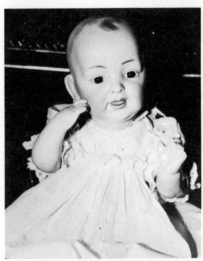

17'' long and 11½'' head circum. Solid dome bisque head with set brown eyes, open/closed mouth and on bent limb baby body. Marks: J.D.K./Made in 12 Germany. This baby also comes with open mouth. Courtesy Mary Sweeney. $395.00.

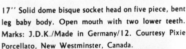

17'' Solid dome bisque socket head on five piece, bent leg baby body. Open mouth with two lower teeth. Marks: J.D.K./Made in Germany/12. Courtesy Pixie Porcellato, New Westminster, Canada.

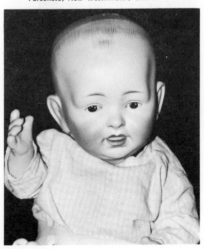

12'' Bisque head on bent leg baby composition body. Painted brown enamel eyes. Open/closed mouth. Marks: J.D.K./Made in Germany. Courtesy Kimport Dolls. $395.00.

KEWPIE

All bisque Kewpies: Standing, one piece body, head and legs, blue wings: 4'' - $85.00, 6'' - $125.00, 8'' - $165.00, 10'' - $250.00, 12'' - $350.00.
All bisque, jointed shoulders and hips: 6'' - $450.00, 8'' - $750.00, 12''-$1,000.00.
Bisque head (glass eyes) on jointed body: 12'' - $3,600.00, 16'' - $4,800.00.
Action Kewpies: All bisque: 4'' - $250.00 - $450.00.

7½'' Rare Kewpie shoulder head with two sew holes in front and back. Cloth body and bisque arms. Has topknot and blue wings on back shoulder. $495.00.

10'' Kewpie (Bisque) Maid of Honor and all original. Human hair wig, with painted eyes to the side. One piece body, head and legs. Jointed shoulders. Also shown are two sizes of the ''Kewpie-Doodle'' dog. Glazed black and white porcelain. The dogs have the Kewpie blue wings. Courtesy Gloyra Woods. 10'' all original: $200.00 - $250.00. Dog: Large - $250.00, Small - $175.00.

103

KEWPIE

Celluloid: 2''-3'' - $25.00, 6'' - $45.00, 8'' - $65.00, 10'' - $75.00, 12'' - 85.00.
Composition: One piece body, legs and head: 12'' - $75.00.
Composition: Jointed shoulders, hips and neck: 12'' - $95.00.
Early vinyl with arms and legs strung: 12'' - $45.00.
Hard plastic with arms and legs strung: 9'' - $65.00, 12'' - $95.00.

22'' Large celluloid Kewpie. Mark: Made in Japan 22, with a fleur de lis. Smaller one is a ''Carnival'' Kewpie that is 13'' tall and of light weight composition. Original red mohair wig, black side glancing eyes, painted on black shoes and socks. Replaced clothes. The larger doll is original. Courtesy Margaret Mandel. Big - $125.00, Small - $50.00.

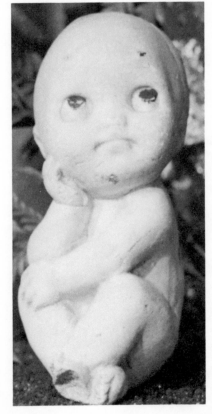

6'' Chalk Kewpie type ''Thinker'', with molded hair, up-turned painted eyes. Marks: ''Some Baby'' Pat. Apl., on back. Courtesy Edith Rollins. Photo by Chuck Pendlebury. $22.00.

KNOCH, GEBRUDER
KO'NIG & WERNICKE

9'' Bisque on five piece, crude mache body with painted on black hose and brown shoes. Marks: G.K./Germany. Made by Gebruder Knoch. Open mouth and set brown eyes. Courtesy Kimport Dolls. $115.00.

14'' Painted over bisque head with open mouth and replaced wig. Blue sleep eyes. Five piece composition body. Marks: K.W./G. GERMANY 136 6/0   Made by Ko'nig & Wernicke.

Courtesy Jil Ashmore. $145.00.

KRUSE, KATHE
LADIES OF FASHION

14½" Kathe Kruse (older) boy with cloth body and mache type material head, painted features and hair. Courtesy Kimport Dolls. 14½" $300.00, 17" -$400.00.

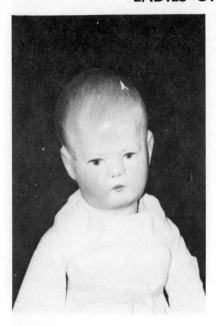

18½" Large Gesland bodied Fashion with F.G. head. (F. Gaultier) Cloth covered body that contains metal pieces and is jointed at hips, knees, shoulders and elbows. Beautiful detail in bisque arms and legs. Swivel bisque head on bisque shoulderplate. Courtesy Kimport Dolls. 16" - $2,300.00, 18½" - $2,750.00.

LADIES OF FASHION

18" Oriental French Fashion with bisque swivel head on bisque shoulder plate. The head has open crown with cork pate. Pierced ears and inset black eyes. Japanese style wig of mohair. Bisque is without colour except for blush marks on cheeks and pale rose lips, which are molded closed and smiling. All leather body without articulation except for gussets at elbows. Marks on lower front corners of shoulder plate could be "E.B.". Originally the doll probably wore a Kimono. Present outfit is contemporary. Courtesy Magda Byfield. (England) $2,500.00.

Shows closeup of Oriental Fashion. Courtesy Magda Byfield.

107

30'' Large Jumeau Fashion with marked Jumeau kid body. Bisque swivel shoulder head on bisque shoulder plate, pierced ears and set blue eyes. Courtesy Kimport Dolls. $3,500.00.

LADIES OF FASHION

11'' F.G. Fashion on French fashion all kid body with leather arms. Closed mouth and set blue eyes. Bisque shoulder plate (swivel neck). All original Lebenon clothes. Courtesy Kimport Dolls. $875.00.

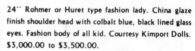

24'' Rohmer or Huret type fashion lady. China glaze finish shoulder head with colbalt blue, black lined glass eyes. Fashion body of all kid. Courtesy Kimport Dolls. $3,000.00 to $3,500.00.

17 ½'' Fashion. Bisque swivel head on bisque shoulder plate, set brown eyes with closed mouth. Kid body with stamp and no other marks: Guillard Pax Infants. The A.T. Guillard company was a wholesaler of toys in Paris from 1842, until the 1860's, when the firm passed into the hands of J.A. Remond. Courtesy Kimport Dolls. $975.00.

LADIES OF FASHION

14" Rohmer Fashion of the 1860's. Bisque head that sits flush with bisque shoulder plate with wire from head (inside) attached to body, so she has a swivel head. China glazed, detailed lower legs and bisque lower arms. Painted blue eyes and closed mouth. Label on chest. Courtesy Kimport Dolls. $3,000.00 to $3,500.00.

13" Fortune Telling Fashion. Intaglio eyes, Pierced ears and closed mouth. Bisque shoulder head on kid body with kid limbs. Has fortune cards under skirt. Marked R.D. Courtesy Kimport Dolls. $1,995.00.

19" French Fashion that has a Belton-type head with concave top and two stringing holes. Open/closed mouth with white area between lips, pierced ears. Has pink wash over eyes. Bisque head on bisque shoulder plate. Marks: 10. Kid fashion body. Courtesy Kimport Dolls. $1,000.00.

110

LEATHER & LENCI

15'' Rare Darrow rawhide leather shoulder head on cloth body with leather arms. Black molded hair. Courtesy Kimport Dolls. $700.00.

17'' Lenci all felt man with mohair glued on hair. Combination of felt and satin outfit. Hat missing. Oil painted features. $125.00.

19'' Lenci. All felt with felt clothes and mohair stitched on wig. Original. Oil painted features with eyes to side. Fingers stitched with free formed thumbs. Courtesy Kimport Dolls. $175.00.

LENCI & TYPES

This page shows part of the Lenci collection of T. Nagawa, Tokyo, Japan. Top left: Shows two girls and a boy. Right is "The Golfer" and the lower photo shows a short Indian, tall Indian Chief and in the center (large doll on chair) sold to Mr. Nagawa, in London, as a Shirley Temple, and extreme right is a beautiful Oriental Lenci, along with a little girl.

Lenci (marked/tagged): Children 16" - $300.00, 22" - $400.00. Golfer: 16" - $450.00, 22" - $600.00. Indian Boy: 16" - $450.00. Indian Chief: 22" -$600.00. Shirley Temple type: 30" - $600.00. Oriental: 16" - $450.00, 22" - $600.00.

LENCI & TYPES

22'' Lenci Bali Dance. All fet with wooden torch stand. Courtesy Kimport Dolls. $350.00.

20'' Felt Lenci-type (not marked) fully jointed with blonde mohair wig. Painted blue eyes with 2nd and 3rd fingers sewn together as in Lenci dolls. Leather shoes, organdy slip and pantaloons, babushka of black rayon with applied flowers, felt skirt. Ca. 1920-1930. Steiff straw stuffed cow 10'' x 6'' with udder and open mouth of pink felt, early mohair covered with black and white glass eyes. C. 1940. Courtesy Margaret Mandel. Doll - $150.00, Cow - $35.00.

25'' Lenci adult with painted open mouth with teeth.
Courtesy Kimport Dolls. $375.00.

LENCI & TYPES

30'' "Bed doll" type Lenci, purchased in London as Marlene Dietrich by owner T. Nagawa, Tokyo, Japan. $350.00.

25'' Lenci Smoker. Jointed knees, removable cigarette. Courtesy Kimport Dolls. $400.00.

10'' Lenci of 1923 and 7½'' Lenci of 1930. Both are all original. Courtesy Gloyra Woods. 10'' - $150.00, 7½'' - $110.00.

LENCI & TYPES

19" Glass eyes Lenci-type. All felt with pin jointed hips and flat stitched fingers. Original. Ca. 1920's. Courtesy Kimport Dolls. $300.00.

18" Chad Valley child. Doll is made out of velvet with mask face, mohair wig and in original dress. She is signed: Chad Valley (England). Courtesy Kimport Dolls. $225.00.

LENCI & TYPES
LERCH & KLAG
LIMOGES

11½'' Lenci-types. These dolls are not marked, but bear a strong resemblence to Lenci dolls. Stitched fingers, felt bodies and clothes. Courtesy Florence Black Musich. 11½'' - $85.00.

25'' Mache of 1875 with Alice in Wonderland hairdo. Cloth body with leather arms. Marks: Lerch and Klag/Manufacturers/Philidelphia, Pa. stamp. Courtesy Kimport Dolls. $995.00.

18½'' Bisque head on composition/mache fully jointed body. Open mouth with sculptured teeth, set brown eyes and pierced ears. Marks: Fabrication/Francaise/ALECo/Limoges/A.F. Courtesy Kimport Dolls. 16'' - $365.00, 18½'' - $475.00, 23'' - $550.00.

LOUISVILLE
MAKER UNKNOWN

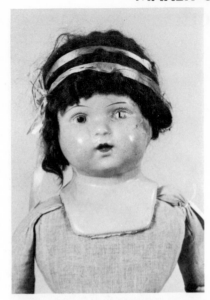

23'' Composition shoulder head and half arms, rest is excelsior filled cloth. Ca. 1920's. Painted features. Marked B.D., on back of shoulder and has a paper label: Louisville Doll & Novelty Mfg. Co. Louisville, KY, in circle and inside circle: KMC/Brand. Courtesy Kimport Dolls. $65.00.

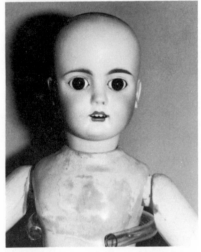

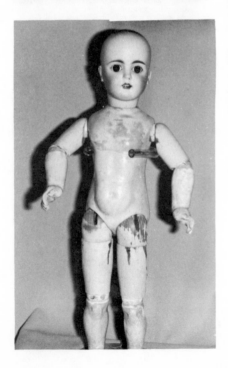

19'' Unknown on mache and wood body. "Roll" necked to take socket head, very "French" looking body except the lower legs, and with so much knee detail, they would appear to be German. The quality and "look" of the head would denote French made as she lacks the German double chin and chin dimple, but it is only a guess. The doll is only marked with a 224. This very same doll in the open/closed mouth version is identical, and the unopened area between the lips is so far apart is appears that the area just had not been cut open to allow for the teeth, and left that way. No matter what the origin of these 224 dolls, they are beautiful and deserve attention. Courtesy Mille Chappelle. $350.00.

MAKER UNKNOWN
BISQUE

8'' Bisque head Oriental child with open mouth and glass eyes. On crude five piece mache body with painted on shoes. Unmarked. $495.00.

5½'' Bisque head Santa on five piece composition body, painted eyes and shoes. No marks. Courtesy Kimport Dolls. $135.00.

5½'' Bisque head with painted eyes and closed mouth. Bald head, and on pin jointed crude mache body and marked Germany. Courtesy Kimport Dolls. $75.00.

5¾'' French type bisque head Groom. Wire armiture body and limbs, crepe paper costume. Bald head with wig. Courtesy Kimport Dolls. $125.00.

MAKER UNKNOWN
BISQUE

16½'' Bisque head on fully jointed French composition body. Closed mouth and set blue eyes. Pierced ears. Marks: B/P 8 G. Body is marked Bebe Jumeau. Courtesy Kimport Dolls. $1,400.00.

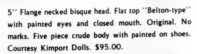

5'' Flange necked bisque head. Flat top ''Belton-type'' with painted eyes and closed mouth. Original. No marks. Five piece crude body with painted on shoes. Courtesy Kimport Dolls. $95.00.

9'' Unmarked Germany with bisque head on five piece composition body and in original riding outfit. Painted on shoes and red hose to knees. Open mouth and sleep eyes. Courtesy Kimport Dolls. $95.00.

MAKER UNKNOWN
BISQUE

28'' Bisque head with bisque shoulder plate (swivel), open/closed mouth with white between lips. Set, almost grey eyes, kid body with long tapered legs and Bru style bisque lower arms. Arms are jointed at the elbows. Marks: 12, on head. Courtesy Kimport Dolls. $1,795.00.

21'' French that resembles the Stiener Bourgoin. Closed mouth with set blue eyes and pink wash over eyes. Pierced ears and has two large cut out areas in back of head at pate (don't know what for) French walker body. Marks: none. Courtesy Kimport Dolls. $1,400.00.

121

MAKER UNKNOWN
BISQUE

24'' Bisque socket head with open mouth and four teeth. Painted lashes below eyes. Marks: 136/11/Made in Germany. This mold number was used by Max Handwerck, but this doll does not appear to have been made by him. Courtesy Clarice Kemper. $275.00.

17½'' Bisque shoulder head on kid body with bisque lower arms. Set brown eyes, open mouth with two upper teeth. Lips are outlined with darker red. Ears are unpierced. Marks: none. Courtesy Kimport Dolls. $185.00.

MAKER UNKNOWN
BISQUE

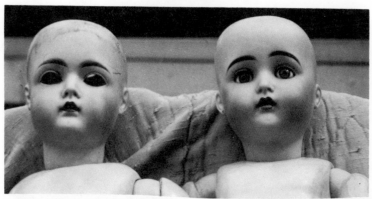

#1 - 20'' - Clean, dressed, wigged; $425.00.

#2 - 20'' - Dressed, wigged; $325.00.

Doll #1 and #2 are both marked 192. The doll on the right (#2) is differently German, and probably by Kestner. Note ''German'' traits: Much knee detail, thinner limbs, less hip area, for example. Doll #1 is different, although head is marked the same. Her body has free formed ball joints, one piece lower arms with solid wrists, and very ''heavy'' compared to the German body, plus being nicely shaped. #1 head is very heavy bisque, the jaws are wider and the bottom lip is curved round and not straight across. The teeth fit up close to the top lip giving it almost a buck tooth look. She has 33 individual lash strokes (Compared with 22, on doll #2) very, very close together. Her brows are very dark brown with a lot of feathering, and the head is wider on the top. We can only quess about doll #1. Courtesy Mary Jane Herzog.

12'' German bisque head with set eyes and open mouth. Composition, fully jointed body with stick legs. All original in off white and deep royal blue. Courtesy Kimport Dolls. $125.00.

MAKER UNKNOWN
BISQUE

29'' Turned shoulder head with closed mouth, set blue eyes and dimple in chin. Cloth body with bisque lower arms. Beautiful quality bisque. Marks: M, high on head. Made in Germany M, low on shoulder plate in back. Courtesy Kimport Dolls. $795.00.

14½'' Slightly turned shoulder head with open mouth, set glass eyes and on kid body with bisque lower arms. Marks: Germany 2015. Courtesy Kimport Dolls. $200.00.

14'' Bisque bald (ball) head that is turned and of very pale bisque. Closed mouth and set eyes. Un-pierced ears. Kid body with bisque lower arms and very delicate modeled fingers. Marks: none. Courtesy Kimport Dolls. $675.00.

MAKER UNKNOWN
BISQUE

11" Bisque head with cloth body and composition lower arms. Sleep glass eyes and closed mouth. Marks: Germany 1925. Courtesy Kimport Dolls. $250.00.

23" Bisque socket head on five piece bent leg baby body. Sleep eyes, open mouth with two molded teeth. This baby is only incised: My Sweet Baby. Courtesy Shirley Smith. $650.00.

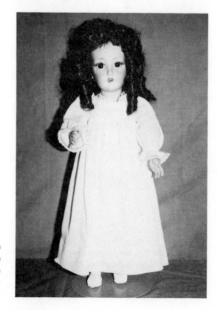

24" Bisque socket head on fully jointed composition body. Sleep eyes, open mouth and a thinner face than most bisque dolls, with thin and "wispy" eyebrows and the lower lashes are painted straight. Courtesy Shirley Smith. $365.00.

MAKER UNKNOWN
CLAY COMPOSITION

11" Denny Dimwit Swayer. All mache of the 1930's.
Courtesy Kimport Dolls. $100.00.

13" Our Pet. Composition socket head on five piece
body with painted features. Original clothes (except
shoes) and wig. Belonged to friend of owners who had
it as a child in 1902. The mouth is closed and she has
a sad expression. Courtesy Jil Ashmore. $110.00.

MAKER UNKNOWN
COMPOSITION

Size unknown Googly with painted eyes to the side. Cloth body with composition head, arms and legs. Doll used in ads for General Electric during 1928.

18" Santa Claus. All composition jointed at neck, shoulders and hips. Molded hat and whiskers. Painted features. No marks. Courtesy A. Pidd Collection. $125.00.

18" Santa Claus in original clothes. The suit is a rust brown, rather than the typical red. Courtesy A. Pidd Collection.

MAKER UNKNOWN
COMPOSITION

20'' Composition shoulder plate with painted blue eyes, replaced wig over molded unpainted hair. Straw stuffed cotton body with calico sewn on shoes, very short composition arms that are nailed on. Doll is unmarked. Ca. 1924. Bear on left: 18'' long mohair Steiff, fully jointed, all straw stuffed, original shoe button eyes, replaced cotton pads and hump re-stuffed. Long and thick feet contour. Ca. 1906. Bear on right: 17'' rose-brown long mohair, original wooden eyes, fully jointed and kapok stuffed, long contoured arms, felt pads. Hardwood discs at joints (very unusual). Ca. 1910-1930. Courtesy Margaret Mandel. Doll: $65.00, Right Bear: $95.00, Left Bear: $175.00.

20'' Unmarked composition shoulder head with composition lower arms. Celluloid over tin sleep eyes, open mouth with two top teeth. Pate slice with cap and red mohair wig. Very tightly stuffed cloth body and limbs. Courtesy Nancy Lucas. $175.00.

Shows the unmarked composition doll undressed. The underwear may be original. Courtesy Nancy Lucas.

MAKER UNKNOWN
COMPOSITION
MELBA
MONTGOMERY, PEGGY

14" Poreous bisque head on jointed body of mache. Sleep blue eyes, open mouth with sculptured teeth. Marks: I H MELBA/3½ England. Courtesy Kimport Dolls. $225.00.

"Baby Peggy" was the daughter of Tom Mix's stand in, Jack Montgomery and as a child of two, three and four, made over 150 two-reel comedies in 1921 and 1922. Her most remembered movie was "Ediths Burglar" in 1925.

20" Baby Peggy. Cloth body with composition head, arms and legs. Molded hair in bangs and "Dutch" bob cut. Painted eyes and closed smiling mouth. Head is a non-swivel shoulder plate. Rare 1923 doll by Louis Amberg. 20" Compo/Cloth - $300.00. 20" Bisque head marked: 1924/L.A. & S.N.Y./Germany/982: $1,500.00.

8½'' high from bottom of shoulder plate to top of head. Brown human hair wig. Metal shoulder head in original box. Marks: Germany 8, on back and on front: Minerva/helmet. Glass eyes. 18'' doll - $85.00. Courtesy of and photo by Clarice Kemper.

METROPOLITAN
NIPPON

21½'' Composition shoulder head girl with molded hair, including molded loop for ribbon. Cloth body with composition arms and legs. Right arm is molded in a bent position. Painted blue eyes, closed mouth. Metropolitan/Doll Co., on shoulder. Courtesy Kimport Dolls. $75.00.

18'' Bisque head on five piece, bent leg baby body. Open mouth and sleep eyes. Marks: F.Y. Nippon. Courtesy Diane Hoffman. 18'' - $225.00.

12'' Bisque socket head on five piece bent leg baby body. Original human hair wig, painted upper lashes, inset blue eyes and open mouth with two teeth. Marks: /No. 76018/Nippon/001. Courtesy Pat Sebastian. 12'' - $145.00. 16'' - $185.00.

23'' Norah Welling's (England) Little Girl. All felt with stitched fingers. Cloth clothes and original. Mohair wig sewn on. Tag: Norah Wellings/England, on foot. (Also see Lenci section.) Courtesy Kimport Dolls. $200.00.

PAPER MACHE

16'' Motschmann type doll with set black glass eyes. Wax over composition with waves painted on each side and the back of the head. Head is jointed at neck. Body is cotton twill, with rest of body wood and composition. Patented April, 1857. Old note attached to doll reads: "this doll was bought in Toronto, Canada in 1860". Courtesy Clarice Kemper. 16'' - $300.00, 20'' - $425.00.

PAPER MACHE

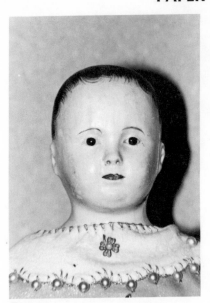

30'' Very early French Paper mache. Ca. 1825. Inset black pupiless glass eyes, painted hair and bamboo teeth. Courtesy Kimport Dolls. $995.00.

4½'' Mache of 1820's. Crude peg jointed wood body and rare hairdo. Courtesy Kimport Dolls. $225.00.

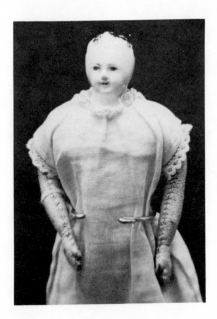

8'' French mache of the 1830's on original kid body, has painted eyes and black painted hair. Courtesy Kimport Dolls. $395.00.

PAPER MACHE

11½'' Mache of the 1830's. Leather body with wooden limbs. Original. Courtesy Kimport Dolls. $595.00.

18'' Early French paper mache Fashion type. Painted blue eyes and painted black pate (no wig). Rigid pink kid body. Ca. 1840. All original. Courtesy Kimport Dolls. $750.00.

19'' Early glass eye paper mache of 1840's. Cloth body with wooden ¾th arms with very long fingers. Hair in braid-bun in back. Courtesy Kimport Dolls. $695.00.

PAPER MACHE

20'' German mache with set brown eyes unusual, open mouth and six teeth. Excelsior (sawdust) filled cloth body with composition limbs. Courtesy Kimport Dolls. $200.00.

14½'' Paper mache shoulder head, with slightly turned head. Original human hair wig, blue glass eyes, cloth stuffed body with mache arms and legs. Black painted shoes, blue ribbed socks, old clothes. Unmarked. Courtesy Margaret Mandel. $125.00.

18'' Paper mache with turned head, glass eyes and closed mouth. Composition lower legs and arms. Front of shoulderplate is marked: Waschecht (washable) and upper right leg: Hotz, next four letters unreadable. Courtesy Nancy Lucas. $185.00.

PAPER MACHE

10½'' All paper mache, jointed at shoulders only. Large painted eyes to the side and molded blonde hair. Original clothes with painted on shoes and sox. Marks: none. Courtesy A.P. Miller Collection. $100.00.

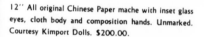

12'' All original Chinese Paper mache with inset glass eyes, cloth body and composition hands. Unmarked. Courtesy Kimport Dolls. $200.00.

10'' Stockenette head with paper mache face mask. "Hug Me" large googly eyes and painted features. One line of hair glued around face. Original green felt costume. Purchased in England. Courtesy Winola Wirt. Photo by Chuck Pendlebury. 10'' - $250.00, 12'' -$350.00.

PAPER MACHE
PARIAN

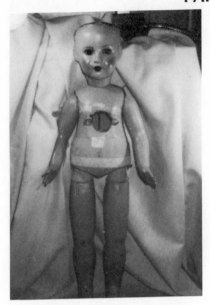

24" Paper mache. Walker with flat feet, all fingers separate and slight curl to arm. Walker mechanism is on a bell shaped wood fastened to legs. Wood pieces in body hold the legs. Sleep rocker eyes with red lashes. Brown eyes with eyeshadow and auburn liner completely around eyes. No marks: Courtesy Marjorie Uhl. $100.00.

Closer look at the 24" paper mache. Shows the cryer box hole in chest and shape of the upper body.

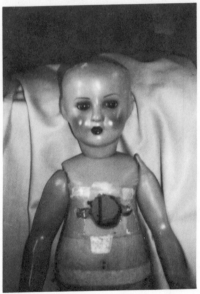

18" Parian with light brown molded hair, exposed ears, and molded on blouse with tie. Painted features. Courtesy Kimport Dolls. $425.00.

PARIAN

21'' Rare black hair Parian with stipple brush marks at temple. Painted blue eyes, snood and applied china glaze shirt top and bow. Cloth body with Parian limbs. Courtesy Kimport Dolls. 21'' Perfect - $750.00, 21'' Repaired - $400.00.

15'' Rare black hair Parian with modeled flowers and yellow necklace. The flowers are blue and white and the Dresden type. Long curls hang down in back with gold trim circles across center of back hairdo. Courtesy Kimport Dolls. 15'' Perfect - $850.00, 15'' Repaired - $495.00.

16'' Empress Eugenia Parian on cloth body with leather arms. The colors of her scarf are very beautiful pastels of pale blue, yellow and pink with gold on the tassel. The snood is black. Courtesy Kimport Dolls. 16'' Perfect - $825.00, 16'' Repaired - $475.00.

PERLE
PUTNAM, GRACE

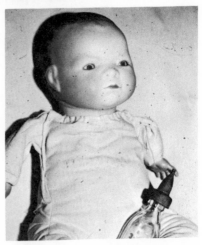

24'' Bisque head with open mouth and teeth sculptured in. Five piece mache body. Marks: Tanagra, in large printed figures and in a diamond/Perle D Epose/10/Paris. This was a trademark by Albert Levy registered in both France (1917) and Germany (1921). Courtesy Kimport Dolls. $695.00.

11½'' long and 10¼'' head. cir. Sleep blue eyes, cloth body with celluloid hands. Red stamp, on body. Marks: Copr. by/Grace S. Putnam/Made in Germany/1393/30. Shows original, and typical Bye-Lo body. Courtesy Mary Sweeney. $350.00.

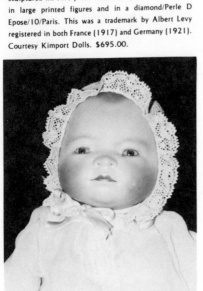

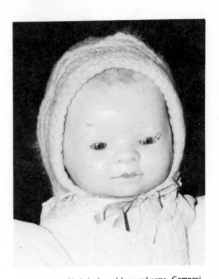

10½'' Bye-Lo with bisque head, tiny blue sleep eyes, cloth body with celluloid hands. Marks: Grace S. Putnam, Copyright. Courtesy Kimport Dolls. $275.00.

16'' Bye-Lo. Cloth body and legs and arms. Composition head with tin sleep blue eyes. Composition gauntlet hands. Marks: Copyright G.S. Putnam. Courtesy Kimport Dolls. $155.00.

RALEIGH
RECKNAGEL

13 ½" Miss Sunshine 1918 Raleigh Doll. (Jessie Mc-Cutcheon Raleigh) All composition with painted features and molded, painted hair. These dolls came as babies, toddlers and children. In the non-baby versions the heads often appear too large for the bodies (in proportions). Courtesy Mildred Hightower. $265.00.

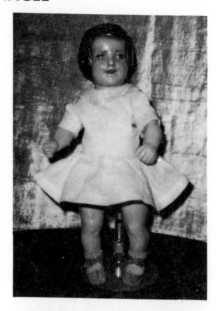

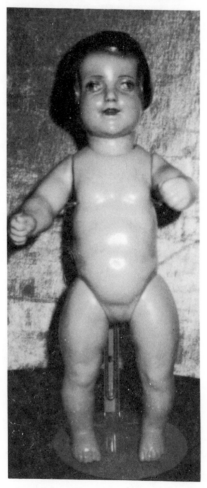

6 ½" Googly on five piece mache body. Molded on hat over molded hair. Intaglio eyes. Marks: R 48 A/12.0. Made by Recknagel of Alexandrinethal. Courtesy Kimport Dolls. $595.00.

RUBBER
SCHORNAU & HOFFMEISTER

16'' Goodyear Rubber doll, painted large blue eyes. Brown with age. Cloth body with leather arms. Courtesy Kimport Dolls. 11½'' - $1,000.00, 16'' -$1,400.00.

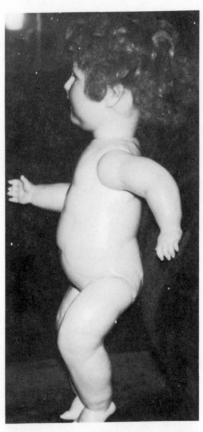

15'' Lightly glazed bisque socket head on five piece bent leg baby body. Sleep eyes with real lashes, plus painted upper and lower lashes. She has an open/closed mouth with two upper teeth. Dimple in chin and feathered eyebrows, and fat double chin. Excellent modeled baby body. Marks: Porzellanfabrik/Burggrub/Das Lachencle Baby/1930-2/Made in Germany/D.R.G.M. Made by Schoenau & Hoffmeister in 1936 through 1931. Distributed by George Borgfelt as "Baby Smiles". The wax looking glaze finish on this doll was perfected in 1929 and put out as "The Laughing Baby" in Germany. Courtesy of a collector from Canada. $365.00 - $425.00.

SCHONEHUT

Boy or girl characters with molded hair/ribbon/comb marks: 14'' - $700.00, 16'' -$850.00.

Pouty, open/closed mouth/painted teeth, or closed mouth: 16'' - $350.00, 19'' -$450.00.

''Baby'', common face, on baby or toddler body: 16'' - $350.00, 17'' - $400.00.

''Dolly'' faced common doll: 16'' - $250.00, 19'' - $350.00.

Same, with sleep eyes: 16'' - $325.00, 19'' - $450.00.

17'' Schonehut girl (middy dress) with wig, painted features and other is 16''. All joints are wire strung. Courtesy JoLeen Flack. 17'' - $350.00-$450.00.

This ad shows a series of Schonehut dolls dressed in the costumes ''of our Allies''. Designed by Jane Porter.

S & C
S & Q
SIMON & HALBIG

Simon & Halbig: with their mark only, not in combination with other markers (example K star R/S & H): "Dolly" face open mouth, kid or compo. Jointed bodies: Example of mold numbers: 130, 550, 1009, 1010, 1039, 1040, 1079, etc.

Allow extra for flirty eyes: 15'' - $265.00, 18'' - $325.00, 22'' - $395.00, 26'' -$450.00, 30'' - $600.00.

Closed Mouth characters such as: 718, 719, 908, 939, 949, etc: 16'' - $850.00, 20'' - $965.00, 25'' - $1,200.00, 28'' - $1,500.00.

Same with open mouths: 16'' - $400.00, 20'' - $495.00, 25'' - $700.00, 28'' -$850.00.

Mold number 1160, referred to as "Little Women": 6'' - $200.00, 9'' - $300.00.

Mold number 1159, 1179 Lady doll open mouth with adult body: 18'' - $850.00, 22'' - $975.00, 25'' - $1,100.00.

Lady doll with closed mouth: 18'' - $2,500.00, 22'' - $3,800.00.

Babies, open/closed mouths. Characters such as 1294, 1428, 1488: 15'' -$1,000.00, 20'' - $1,500.00.

25'' Bisque socket head on fully jointed composition body. Sleep blue eyes, pierced ears and open mouth with three teeth. Molded, painted eyebrows. Marks: S & C Simon & Halbig/62. Made by Simon & Halbig for Sannier & Caut. Courtesy Jackie Barker. $425.00.

24'' with 17'' head cir. life size baby. On five piece bent leg baby body. Blue sleep eyes, open mouth and very pale bisque. Body is stamped Germany and head is marked: S Q (interwoven)/14/Germany. Made by Schuetzmeister & Quendt. Courtesy Gloyra Woods. $435.00.

24'' Bisque head with flirty eyes/lashes and open mouth marked: Simon Halbig/S & H/Germany/11 ½. Is on a French walker body of composition with kid covered torso. Large key in lower torso to operate walker mechanism. Key is marked R.D. Courtesy Kimport Dolls. $595.00.

SIMON & HALBIG

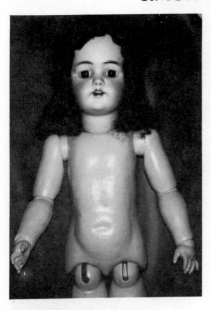

26'' Excellent bisque socket head on fully jointed composition body. Sleep eyes, open mouth, molded brows and pierced ears. Marks: 1078 Germany/Simon & Halbig S & H 12. Courtesy Pixie Porcellato, New Westminister, Canada.

25'' Bisque socket head on fully jointed composition body. Open mouth, pierced ears, sleep eyes. Excellent quality bisque. Marks: S & H 1079/DEP/Germany/11. Courtesy Pixie Porcellato, New Westminister, Canada.

8'' Bisque socket head with original mohair wig. On five piece composition body with painted on red shoes. Sleep eyes, open mouth that is so narrow there were never any teeth. Marks: 1078/S & H/Germany. Courtesy Millie Chappell. 6'' - $150.00, 8'' -$175.00, 9'' - $195.00.

SMITH, P.D.

20'' P.D. Smith doll of composition open mouth with two lower teeth and flirty glass eyes. Body is jointed at neck, shoulders, hips and wrists. Dolls are marked with an ''S'', under the wig and near the dome section fitting over the head opening. Mr. & Mrs. Putnam David Smith made dolls from 1913 to 1922 at their home in Santa Clara, Calif. Their daughter, Margaret Smith, helped with the dolls. Mrs. Smith's given name was Mabel. This doll was made about 1918 and is the property of Gladys Prescott, niece of Mabel & Puttnam Smith, and is on loan in the collection of Faye Blazek. $650.00.

SOCIETE FRANCAISE de FABRICATION de BEBES et JOUETS (S.F.B.J.) SNOW BEAR

Snow Babies: Textured bisque, in many action positions painted features, excellent quality: on sled, with dog, etc: 3'' - $55.00, 4½'' - $75.00. Jointed shoulders and/or legs: 4'' - $150.00. Action, but poor quality: 3'' - $25.00, 4½'' - $35.00.

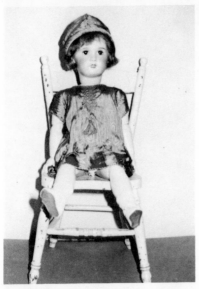

30'' Late bisque socket head on fully jointed mache and wood body. Open mouth and sleep eyes. Marks: S.F.B.J. Courtesy Erma Beaty. 16'' - $400.00, 22'' -$500.00, 24'' - $695.00, 30'' - $895.00.

8½'' French World War I Nurse. Bisque head with mache five piece body, with painted on black boots. She is all original except has replaced head gear. Wig is original. Eyes are painted. Marks: SFBJ/60/Paris/13/0. Courtesy Jil Ashmore. $125.00

3¼'' Snow bear. All good quality porcelain bisque with ''snow'' covering. Note well modeled feet. Made in Germany. Courtesy Phyllis Houston. $55.00.

STEINER, JULES

18½'' Mechanical Steiner with a different "look". Open mouth with tiny teeth. Key wind, kicks, crys, moves arms and head. Set blue eyes with pink wash over them. Courtesy Kimport Dolls. $1,375.00.

12'' Bisque head on fully jointed composition and wood body. Closed mouth and sleep eyes, operated by wires through back of head. Called "Wire-eye Steiner". Marked Bourgoin-Steiner. Courtesy Kimport Dolls. $2,495.00.

22'' Wax over mache Steiner mechanical doll that is key wound and cries, turns head, eyes close and open and moves arms and legs. Tuffts of painted hair on sides and in back, plus wig. Open mouth with two upper and two lower teeth. Courtesy Kimport Dolls. $1,250.00.

26'' Jules Steiner with closed mouth and set blue eyes. Pierced ears and on fully jointed French mache and composition body. Marks: Steiner/Paris/Fire A 15. Courtesy Kimport Dolls. 26'' Perfect - $3,000.00, 26'' Hairline -$1,995.00.

SWAINE & CO.
SUPERIOR

19½" Lori baby marked 232 by S & C (Swaine & Co/Germany). Open mouth with tongue and two lower teeth. Unusual in this size. Bent leg baby body, arms jointed at wrist and right arm bent at elbow, very large hands. Courtesy Kimport Dolls. $950.00.

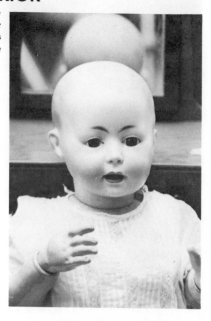

14½" Superior Doll with label on back of shoulder. Cloth body with leather arms. Blonde sausage curls. Courtesy Kimport Dolls. $225.00.

WAX

9'' Wax over mache "pumpkin head" of 1880. Inset eyes, cloth body with wooden legs. Surely she had a wig once! Courtesy Kimport Dolls. $110.00.

11'' Rare wax of the 1840's. Peg jointed wooden body and limbs. Inset glass eyes and slot on top of head for wig. Courtesy Kimport Dolls. $1,695.00.

17 ½'' Wax Creche women with inset glass eyes, closed mouth and wood padded body. Wax arms and carved wooden feet with sandals. Molded hair. Courtesy Kimport Dolls. $400.00.

WAX

25" German wax over mache of 1885. Cloth body with composition limbs (modeled on boots) and glass eyes. Courtesy Kimport Dolls. $275.00.

20" Wax over mache of the 1880's. Cloth body that is sawdust filled. Wax over mache limbs with molded on high top boots. Set blue eyes, closed mouth. Pierced ears. Courtesy Kimport Dolls. $165.00.

26" English wax with slit top in head to embed wig. Glass pupiless eyes, cloth body and blue leather arms. Courtesy Kimport Dolls. $325.00.

WAX

28'' German pumpkin wax with inset eyes, blonde molded curls and painted ribbon and bow. Cloth body with wooden limbs. Pierced ears. Courtesy Kimport Dolls. $300.00.

20'' German wax over mache of the early 1900's. Open mouth and glass eyes. Cloth body with composition lower arms. Courtesy Kimport Dolls. $95.00.

10'' Beautifully made wax doll that is poured wax over paper mache. Instead of legs there is a small box for jewels or treasures. Courtesy Carole Noe. $75.00.

10'' Poured wax over mache with upper torso wax and instead of legs there is a box. Beautifully gowned. Date unknown. Courtesy Carole Noe. $75.00.

WEBBER
WELSCH

26'' Webber Singing Wax of 1880. Marked on hip. Handle to wind is on side and Victolia mechanism in the lower front. The cylinder in this one is ''London Bridges''. Set blue eyes and closed mouth. Courtesy Kimport Dolls. $795.00.

19'' Bisque socket head on mache/wood fully jointed body that is marked Made in France in a square. Pale bisque with sleep eyes and open mouth. Marks:  200/Welsch/Made in Germany. Made for Max Oscar Arnold. Courtesy Pixie Porcellato, New Westminister, Canada. $325.00.

9'' Bisque socket head on five composition body with molded, painted on shoes and socks. Sleep eyes and open mouth. Marks: Welsch MOA, on head. Made for Max Oscar Arnold. Courtesy Lilah Beck. $145.00.

WHITE BISQUE
WOOD

10½" White bisque with molded hair of the 1870's. Cloth body with white bisque lower arms and legs. Painted on black boots. Courtesy Kimport Dolls. $150.00.

16" Bisque shoulder head on cloth body with bisque lower arms. Set brown eyes, closed mouth and molded blonde hair. Marks: none. Courtesy Kimport Dolls. $85.00.

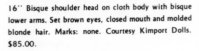

16" Primitive wood of the 1850's. Cloth body with wooden 3/4th arms with spoon hands. Unusual hairdo. Courtesy Kimport Dolls. $395.00.

DIRECTORY OF DOLL MARKS

The following marks may be found incised on certain doll's heads, and this list will give you a quick reference so you can give the mark further research.

A.B. & Co. . . . Althof, Bergmann & Co.

A.B.G.: In script/intertwined . . . . Alt, Beck & Gottschalk

A.M. . . . . Armand Marseille

A & M . . . . . . M.J. Moehling, Austria

Amour Bebe . . . . Louis Guillet

Anchor, plus A.L. - or A.L. & Cie . . . . . A. Lanternier & Cie

A & S . . . . Abraham & Strauss Co.

A.T. . . . . A. Thuillier

A.W. in triangle . . . . . . Adolf Wislizinus

Baby Betty . . . . Armand Marseille

Baby Phyllis . . . . Armand Marseille

Baby Ruth . . . . Craemer & Heron of Sonneburg

Baby Stuart . . . . Gebruder Heubach

Bavaria & crown . . . . William Gobel

Bebe A.L. . . . . Alexandre Lefebvre

Bebe Charmant . . . . . Pintel & Godchaux

Bebe Cosmopolite . . Heinrich Handwerck

Bebe Phenix . . . . Henri Alexandre

Bebe Reclame . . . . . Heinrich Handwerck

Bertha . . . . Hertwig & Co.

B.F. . . . . Ferte

B.P. & crossed swords . Bahr & Proschild

B.P. in heart . . . . Bahr & Proschild

B.S. . . . . Bruno Schmidt

B.S.W. inside a heart . . . . Bruno Schmidt

BTE . . . . . . Means Brevete, French word meaning "Patented".

Buporit . . . . Barh & Proschild

Catterfelder Carl Troutman of Catterfelder Puppenfabrik

Cirlce dot . . . . Bru

C.M.B. . . . . Charles M. Bergmann

C.O.D. . . . . Cuno & Otto Dressel

C.P. . . . . Mme Pannier, also Kestner

Darling Baby . . . . Armand Marseille

Deponiert . (Dep.) German mark meaning "Registration".

Depose . . . . French mark meaning "Registration".

Deutshe Geschaft . . . . (D.G.) means German made.

Diana . . . . Alfred Heller

DKF . . . . Dernheim, Koch & Fisher

Dolly Dimples . . . Hamburger & Co., or Gebruber Heubach.

DR . . . . Deutches Reich (Germany)

DRGM . . . . . for an incorporated German Company or registered design (Deutsches Reichs Gebrauchs Muster).

Dotter . . . . Bawo & Dotter

Duchess . . . . Armand Marseille

E.D. . . . . E. Denamur

Eden Bebe . . . . Fleischmann & Blodel

Edwina . . . . Louis Amberg

E.I.H. . . . . Horsman Doll

Einco . . . . Eisenmann & Co.

E.J. . . . . Jumeau

E.U.S.t, in triangle . . . . . Edmond Ulrich Steiner

Fany . . . . Armand Marseille

F.G. . . . . Fernand Gaultier

Flordora . . . . Armand Marseille

F.S. & Co. . . . . Fran Schmidt & Co.

G . . . . Gera

G.B. . . . . George Borgfelt

Ges. Gesch. (Gesetzlich geschutzt) means Registered or Patented.

Globe Baby . . . . Carl Hartman

Goss . . . . . William Goss of Staffordshire

Grete . . . . Otto Reinecke

G.S. . . . . Gans & Seyfarth

G & S . . . . Gebruder Sussenguth

H, with S inside . . . . Herman Steiner

Handwerck . Both Heinrich and Max used

Hanna . . . . Schoenau & Hoffmeister

Harmus . . . . Carl Harmus

HcH . . . . Heinrich Handwerck

H & Co. . . . . Hamburger & Co.
Henry a la Pensee, Paris . Paris Toy Shop
Herzi . . . . Otto Reinecke
Heubach, in square . . Gebruder Heubach
Hilda . . . . J.D. Kestner
Holz Masse Name of wood pulp and used
 by Cuno & Otto Dressel.
Horseshoe . . . . Heubach Kopplesdorf
J.D.K. . . . . J.D. Kestner
Jullien . . . . Jullien Jeune
Juno with crown . . . . Karl Standfuss
Just Me . . . . Armand Marseille
Jutta . . . . Cuno & Otto Dressel
K, in bell . . . . Kling & Co.
Kiddie Joy . . . . Armand Marseille
K & H, in banner . . . . Kley & Hahn
K & K . . . . Kahl & Kohle
Knobbi-Kid . . . . Armand Marseille
KPM . . . . Koeniglicke Porzellen
K & R, with 6 point star . . . . . Kammer
 & Reinhart
K & W . . . . Ko'nig & Wernicke
M.B., in circle . . . Morimura Bros. Japan
Mejestic . . . . Edmund Ulrich Steiner
Mascotte . . . . May Freres
MH . . . . Max Handwerck
Minerva, with helmet . . . Bushow & Beck
M.J.C. . . . . Martha Chase
My Girlie . . . . George Borgfelt
My Playmate . . . . Armand Marseille
M & S Superior . . . Muller & Strassburger
Queen Louise . . . . Armand Marseille
Paris Bebe . . . . Danel & Cie
Pet Name China (Pauline, Helen, etc) . .
 Hertwig & Co.
P.M. . . . . Otto Reinecke

P.S. . . . . Phillip Samhammer & Co.
P.S., in circle or P.Sch., in oval . . . . Paul
 Schmidt
P.Sch. . . . . Peter Scherf
R.A. . . . . . . Rechnagel of Aleandrinethal
Raynal . . . . Raynal of Paris
R.D. . . . . Rabery & Delphieu
Revalo . . . . Gebruder Ohlhaver
RH, in circle with swan . . . Robert Hiller
 & Co.
Roseland . . . . Armand Marseille
S & C . . . . Sannier & Caut
Santa . . . . Simon & Halbig
Sch, and crossed swords, inshield Schmitt
 & Fils
Schultz Marke . . . Rheinsche Gumme und
 Celluloid Fabrik Co.
S.F.B.J. . Societe Francaise de Fabrication
 de Bebe et Jouels
S.G.D.G. . . . . means ''Sana garantie du
 gouverement'' (without guarantee of the
 government).
S & H . . . . Simon and Halbig
Shuco . . . . Schreyer & Co.
S Pb in star H . . Schoenau & Hoffmeister
S & Q . . . . Schuetzmeister & Quendt
Stork . . . . Parsons and Jackson
Three leaf clover with L & numbers inside
 leaf . . . . Limbach Porzellanfabrik
Trebor . . . . Otto Reinecke
Turtle in diamond Rheinische Gummi und
 Celluloid Fabrik Co.
Unis . . . . Union Natioale Inter-Syndicali
Walkure . . . . Kley and Hahn
W.G. intertwined . . . . . . William Gobel
W & Z . . . . Wagner & Zetsche

MODERN AND NEWER DOLLS

11½-Inch
FASHION DOLL
With Wardrobe
$4.99
See page 9
1
White or
Colored

✓ Party Dress
✓ Coat-Dress
✓ Country Outfit

2
BIG AS LIFE
30-Inch
Toddler **$4.99**
See page 9

3
"PRETTY POLLY"
In Choice of 3 Outfits
25-In. **$5.99**
See page 9

White or
Colored

new wonderful dream **DOLLS**

White or
Colored

5
25-Inch
**DRINK 'N
WET BABY**
$4.49
See page 9

25-Inch
**NEWBORN
BABY**
$5.99
See page 9
7

6
**SNOWSUIT
BABY**
$3.99 Up
See page 9

White or
Colored

23-Inch
WALKER
$4.99
See page 9
8

BRIDE DOLL
$2.99 Up
See page 9
10

White
or Colored

4
Life Size "Debbie"
**THREE-FOOT
WALKER**
$9⁹⁸
See page 9
6

White or
Colored

9
25-Inch
BABY DOLL
$2.99 See page 9

A & H

The dolls from the A & H Doll Co., Dutchess Dolls, any of the dolls from the 1950's (although some are even made today) were very popular and sold through outlets such as Montogomery Wards, Sears & Roebuck, etc. They were very reasonably priced dolls, and are referred to by collectors as "Dime dolls". They will never become extremely fine dolls to collect, because of various reasons. Some of these reasons are: too many of them are of poor quality, especially the clothes, as they are glued or stapled onto the doll, each doll is the same, only the clothes may be different, there are too many of the dolls around. But, no matter why they are not highly collectable, they deserve a place in doll books as they are part of the doll history.

7 ½" Marcie Doll. All hard plastic with sleep blue eyes. Mohair wig. One piece body and legs. This is the Alice In Wonderland with blue satin dress and white apron with red trim. Wonder Book published in 1951. Dress tag: This is a/Marcie/Doll. Box: A Marcie Read & Play Creation. A Marcie/Lovely Alice/Creation. $8.00.

8" "Irene Bride". All hard plastic with glued on brown wig, sleep eyes. Painted on shoes. Marks: tag: this is a/Marcie Doll. 1952. $3.00.

160

ALEXANDER

The first of these dolls were 7½ '' tall and were straight leg, non walkers (1953-1954) Some of these very early dolls were ''Quiz-kins'' with ''yes'' and ''no'' buttons in the middle of the back. The dolls became 8'' tall in 1955 and were then straight leg, walker, and their heads turned as they walked. In 1956 the dolls were 8'' and now had bending knees and were still a walker. They remained jointed knee walkers until 1966, when the walker mechanism was dis-continued. (They still had jointed knees). In 1973 the dolls once again became straight leg, non walkers. The first straight leg, non walking dolls are of much better quality, are heavier, where the later ones have a ''powdery'' look about them and seam lines that have not been cleaned off well.

8'' Alexander-kin/Wendy dressed in #458-1955. She is a straight leg, walker and wears a white organdy pinafore over pink organdy dress. Courtesy Pat Spirek. $95.00.

Alexander-kin/Wendy Ann prices based on:	Short dress	Ball gown
Mint, including shoes and sox	$75.00	$100.00
Clean, played with, but all original	$55.00	$ 75.00
Hair mussed, original clothes washed	$40.00	$ 60.00
No original clothes, but dressed and clean	$35.00	$ 35.00
Nude doll, hair in fair condition	$30.00	$ 30.00

Add $25.00 more to early straight leg, non walker. Add $25.00 more to straight leg, walker. The following is a list of the Alexander-kin dolls that have been dis-continued. The first price is for a mint, unplayed with doll. The second price is for a doll that is dirty, played with, or part of original clothes gone.

African	$225.00	$85.00
Amish Boy or Girl	$300.00	$75.00
Argentine Boy	$300.00	$75.00
Bolivia	$200.00	$75.00
Ecuador	$350.00	$75.00
Eskimo	$350.00	$85.00
Hawaiian	$200.00	$85.00
Greek Boy	$200.00	$75.00
Indian Boy	$350.00	$85.00
Indian Girl	$350.00	$85.00
Korea	$300.00	$85.00
Morocco	$300.00	$75.00
Miss U.S.A.	$250.00	$75.00
Peruvian Boy	$300.00	$75.00
Spanish Boy	$300.00	$75.00
Vietnam	$300.00	$75.00

Add $50.00 for ''Maggie Face'' on mint doll. Add $20.00 for ''Maggie Face'' on dirty doll.

ALEXANDER

BABIES	Mint & Original	Played with, or dirty & not original
Little Genuis, compo, 20''	$ 85.00	$20.00
Baby McGuffey, compo, 20''	$125.00	$45.00
Pinky, compo, 23''	$ 75.00	$20.00
Prescious, compo, 12''............	$ 65.00	$20.00
Slumbermate, compo, 12''	$ 95.00	$40.00
Cookie, compo, 19''	$ 95.00	$35.00
Princess Alexandria, 24''	$ 95.00	$20.00
Sunbeam, vinyl, 16''.............	$ 85.00	$30.00
Honeybun, vinyl, 23''............	$ 75.00	$20.00
Bonnie, vinyl, 19''	$ 65.00	$20.00
Kathy, vinyl, 15 ''...............	$ 55.00	$15.00
Genuis, vinyl, flirty eyes...........	$ 65.00	$30.00
Lively Huggums, vinyl, 25''	$ 65.00	$20.00
Littlest Kitten, vinyl, 8''	$ 95.00	$25.00
Happy, vinyl, 20''	$ 85.00	$25.00

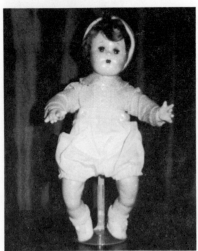

11'' Butch. Cloth body with composition head and limbs. Comes with wig, or molded hair. Tag: "Butch" Madame Alexander/N.Y. U.S.A./All Rights Reserved. Original. Courtesy A.P. Miller. $85.00.

10'' Cissette in flowered formal with velveteen long stole that is rose color. Inside of stole matches gown. Courtesy Pat Spirek. $150.00.

Cissette in street dresses, with hat if one came with outfit, shoes and hose, mint -$135.00, played with - $50.00. Cissette in ball gown, mint - $200.00, played with -$65.00. Cissette face Portrettes: Queen, mint - $200.00, dirty, played with - $75.00. Southern Bell, mint - $300.00, dirty, played with - $65.00. Scarlett, mint - $250.00, dirty, played with - $35.00. Jacqueline doll, mint $250.00, dirty, played with - $50.00.

ALEXANDER

10" Cissette as "Gold Rush" - 1963. Has the "Margot" style hairdo and makeup, using the Cissette doll. A very rare doll. Courtesy Mary Williams. $850.00 up.

15" Cynthia. 1952. All hard plastic and original. This dress came in various colors. (Margaret face). Courtesy Mary Williams. $450.00.

17" Dionne Quints. All composition, sleep eyes and closed mouths. All original. Marks: Dionne/Alexander. Courtesy Erma Beaty, Canada. $135.00 each, $800.00 set.

Dionne Quints

	Mint & Original	Played with, Not original	Mint set Of five
8" Toddlers,	$95.00	each, $20.00	$ 550.00
11" baby,	$165.00	each, $35.00	$ 900.00
11" Toddler,	$175.00	each, $35.00	$ 950.00
14" Toddler,	$200.00	each, $40.00	$1,200.00
16" Toddler,	$225.00	each, $50.00	$1,300.00
19" Toddler,	$275.00	each, $70.00	$1,500.00

ALEXANDER

Elise: (1957-1960, 16½ '' only)

	Mint & Original	Played with not all original
Street dress	$150.00 up	$45.00
Ball gown	$175.00 up	$45.00
Mary-bel head	$150.00	$55.00
Ballerina	$165.00	$50.00
Bride	$165.00	$50.00

16½'' Elise. Hard plastic with vinyl over-sleeved arms and jointed at the elbows. Jointed ankles, so feet can be ''flat'' or ''high-heeled''. All original. Courtesy Rita DiMare. $150.00.

7'' Quintuplets. Vinyl body and limbs with hard plastic heads. Open mouth/nursers. (Little Genuis) called Fischer Quints by collectors. 1964. Majority of these dolls came in a diaper only. These have been redressed. Courtesy Mary Williams. $50.00 each, $300.00 set.

ALEXANDER

17" Flora McFlimsey of Madison Square, and so tagged. All composition with open mouth and freckles. Human hair wig and original in yellow with brown trim. Doll is marked: Princess Elizabeth. Courtesy A.P. Miller. 17" - $200.00. 22" - $225.00 mint, original - $85.00 in fair condition. 15" - $175.00 mint, original - $60.00 in fair condition. 12" - $165.00 mint, original - $50.00 in fair condition. 15" 1953 Cissy - $250.00, mint - $75.00 in played with condition.

18" Godey of 1953. All hard plastic using the large eyed Maggie mold. All original. Brown sleep eyes. Grey fur cape. Courtesy Pam Ortman. Any of the Maggie, Margaret and Cissy face dolls used for early portraits or special doll, if mint and all original, $250.00-$350.00. Dusty, dirty, messed up clothes $100.00.

ALEXANDER

17'' Leslie. (Black Polly). 1965 to 1971. In beautiful blue ball gown and blue ribbon in rooted hair. Sleep brown eyes. All original. Courtesy Mary Williams.

Bride	$145.00 Mint	$45.00 Fair
Ball gown	$175.00 Mint	$75.00 Fair
Ballerina	$125.00 Mint	$45.00 Fair
Street dress	$125.00 Mint	$45.00 Fair

12'' Lissy Bridesmaid #1161-1957. Blue nylon gown and hat. All original. Courtesy Pat Spirek.

Bridesmaid or Bride	$150.00 Mint	$70.00 Fair
Street dress	$150.00 Mint	$50.00 Fair
Ballerina	$145.00 Mint	$65.00 Fair
Ball gown	$200.00 Mint	$75.00 Fair

Specials, such as Southern Belle, McGuffey Ana, etc., Mint $750.00 up, Fair condition, but original $200.00 up.

14'' Little Colonel. All composition with sleep eyes and closed mouth (Betty). Doll is unmarked. Clothes Tagged: Madame Alexander. All original. Courtesy Pat Spirek.

9''	$200.00 Mint	$ 60.00 Fair
11''-13''	$350.00 Mint	$ 75.00 Fair
18''	$450.00 Mint	$ 85.00 Fair
23''	$450.00 Mint	$100.00 Fair
27''	$550.00 Mint	$125.00 Fair

ALEXANDER

8'' Little Lady. 1960 and using the Maggie Mixup faced doll. In aqua blue with blue and rose on white pinafore. Bend knee walker. Came in a plastic frame along with toiletries. Courtesy Pat Spirek. Mint -$300.00, Original, but dirty - $95.00.

15'' Little Women using the Maggie face and also the Margaret face dolls from 1948-9 into the 1950's. Some sets measure 14'' also. Prices are based on the doll being in good condition and all original and tagged: $150.00, except the ''Jo'' with long loop curls around the back of the head, her price is: $175.00. 15'' Set - $850.00. 8'' Walkers, straight leg-walker - $125.00 each. 12'' (Lissy) - $200.00 each. Laurie -$500.00. 12'' Plastic and vinyl (Mary Ann) - Still available. 7'' Composition - $100.00 each. 9'' Composition - $125.00 each. 13''-15'' Composition -$165.00 each.

8'' Maggie Mixup. #599-1960 with variation of color and print of apron used. All hard plastic and bend knee, walker. Orange-red straight hair, green sleep eyes and freckles. This is the ''regular'' Wendy/Alexander-kin head used for Maggie Mixup and a new head was also designed with smile mouth and smaller eyes. (See Little Lady). Smile mouth -$200.00, Wendy face - $200.00.

ALEXANDER

18'' Margaret O'Brien. All composition, glued on dark red wig with pigtails looped and tried with ribbon, blue sleep eyes. All original, except pin. Dress is blue, but came also in pink and yellow. Marked Alexander. Courtesy Gloyra Woods. 14½'' - $490.00, 21'' -$500.00, 18'' - $450.00, 18'' Hard plastic -$400.00.

17'' Polly #1751-1965. Permanent pleated tulle (pink) skirt with pink sequined bodice. Courtesy Mary Williams.

Bride	$125.00 Mint	$35.00 Fair
Ball gown	$150.00 Mint	$50.00 Fair
Street Dress	$125.00 Mint	$35.00 Fair
Ballerina	$125.00 Mint	$35.00 Fair

ALEXANDER

21'' Queen and 10'' Queen. (Cissy and Cissette).
21'' In white - $275.00, In gold - $225.00. 10''
-$200.00.

CISSY

In ballgown	$225.00 up		
	Mint	$ 85.00 Fair	
As Bride	$145.00 Mint	$ 60.00 Fair	
Bridesmaid	$145.00 Mint	$ 70.00 Fair	
Street dresses	$135.00 Mint	$ 45.00 Fair	
Miss Flora			
McFlimsey	$250.00 Mint	$100.00 Fair	
Portrait			
(Godey,etc)	$500.00 Mint	$150.00 Fair	
Scarlett O'Hara	$400.00 Mint	$150.00 Fair	

18'' Scarlett O'Hara. All composition with black
mohair wig, green sleep eyes. Gown is brown with
white collar and green trim, hat and sash. The following prices are for mint and original composition dolls.
The second price is for played with doll with light craz-
ing and the third price is for badly damaged composition, but original.

7''	$250.00	$100.00	$40.00
9''-11''	$275.00	$ 85.00	$45.00
13''-14''	$225.00	$ 85.00	$45.00
16''-17''	$250.00	$ 95.00	$60.00
18''-19''	$350.00	$110.00	$85.00
21''	$400.00	$125.00	$95.00

ALEXANDER

14'' Sonja Henie. All composition with sleep eyes and open mouth/teeth. Pink satin skating dress, gold skates. Marks: Madame Alexander/Sonja/Henie, on head. 1940. Courtesy Kimport Dolls. 14'' - $175.00, 18'' - $250.00, 21'' - $300.00.

This is the SMALL set of Sound of Music dolls. The dolls measures from 8'', 10'', and 12''. The Large set measures 11'', 14'' and 17''. The small set was made from 1971 to 1973 and the large set from 1965 to 1970. The following prices are based on mint and original dolls, with the second price for played with, but original dolls.

SMALL SET			LARGE SET		
8'' Friedrich	$ 85.00	$ 40.00	11'' Friedrich	$ 125.00	$ 50.00
8'' Gretl	$ 85.00	$ 40.00	11'' Gretl	$ 125.00	$ 50.00
8'' Marta	$ 85.00	$ 40.00	11'' Marta	$ 125.00	$ 50.00
10'' Brigitta	$ 125.00	$ 65.00	14'' Brigitta	$ 150.00	$ 65.00
10'' Louisa	$ 250.00	$100.00	14'' Louisa	$ 200.00	$ 75.00
10'' Liesl	$ 200.00	$ 75.00	14'' Liesl	$ 150.00	$ 75.00
12'' Maria	$ 150.00	$ 75.00	17'' Maria	$ 175.00	$ 75.00
Complete small set	$1,100.00	$500.00	Complete large set	$1,200.00	$500.00

The very first LARGE set of Sound of Music dolls also were available in sailor suits (all seven dolls). The prices for ones dressed in sailor outfits is unrecordable as there are no prices to base their values on.

AMERICAN CHARACTER

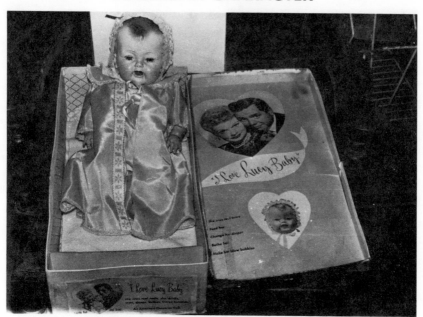

16'' Lucy Baby (early) All rubber body and limbs. Hard plastic head with sleep eyes/lashes. The eyes are ''squinted'' and has tear ducts in the corners. Excellent quality. palms are down and all fingers separate. The doll resembles a Tiny Tears (except for the eyes). The box is marked American Character. It is assumed that the doll is marked American Character. It is assumed that the doll was put on the market before the actual ''birth'' of Ricky on the T.V. Show. One owner's box was autographed by Desi Arnez, and the owner has a letter from Lucille Ball, but neither Desi, nor Lucy had heard of this doll. It is not reasonable to assume the doll was meant to be the Arnez's first born, daughter , as she was not ''publicized'' as part of the T.V. show at all, and was actually born before the popularity of the show. Doll, courtesy Marion Dutton, and some information courtesy Cookie Mullen. In Box -$00.00, Nude - $00.00.

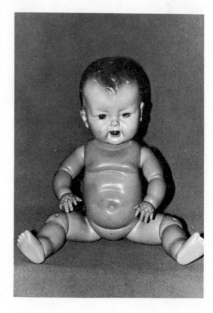

This shows the ''I Love Lucy'' baby undressed. It has a very character face with ''squinted'' eyes. Undressed but in excellent condition - $65.00, Body damaged, meduim condition - $35.00, Body in bad condition -$15.00.

AMERICAN CHARACTER

The "Sweet Sue" dolls were made from 1950 through the late 1950's. The first were all hard plastic, then hard plastic with vinyl heads and then all vinyl. A great many are unmarked, but if they are they will be marked: A.C., Amer. Char. Doll, or American Character and a date in a circle.

Hard plastic, 14'' mint - $45.00, played with, dirty - $20.00. Mint, 18'' - $60.00, played with, dirty - $30.00.

Hard plastic/vinyl, 14'' mint - $40.00, played with - $15.00. 18'' mint - $55.00, played with $25.00.

All vinyl, 10½'' mint - $35.00, played with, dirty - $10.00. 17'' mint - $45.00, played with, dirty - $20.00. 21'' mint - $65.00, played with, dirty - $30.00. 25'' mint - $100.00, played with, dirty - $45.00.

18'' Godey Lady by American Character using the Sweet Sue Doll of all hard plastic. No marking on doll. Red-brown hair is braided with extra braided hair piece. Walker, head turns as she walks. All original except necklace. 1956. Courtesy Donnie Durant. $60.00.

30'' Miss Echo. Plastic and vinyl with rooted hair, blue sleep eyes and open/closed mouth with painted teeth. Battery operated talker with recorder that plays back for ½ minute and erases automatically. On and off knob on upper chest. In one of her original dresses. 1963 and unmarked. Made by American Character. Courtesy June Schultz. $75.00.

AMERICAN CHARACTER

24" Babie Babbles. Cloth with vinyl head and limbs. Uses the same head as Sally Says. Marks: American Doll & Toy Corp./1964. Courtesy Doris Richardson. $55.00.

19" Sally Says. Plastic and vinyl. Battery operated talker. Marks: American Doll & Toy Corp./1964. Original. Courtesy Doris Richardson. $50.00.

19" Pittie Pat. Plastic and vinyl. All original. Used same head as does the Sally Says, Butterball, Babie Babbles and others. Mechanism makes "Heart Beat" sounds. Marked American Doll & Toy/1964. Courtesy Doris Richardson. $60.00.

AMERICAN CHARACTER

14" Sweet Sue. All hard plastic, walker, head turns. All original in original box. Shoes snap on both sides. 1953. Marked A.C., on head. $40.00.

23" Toodles with "follow me eyes" called "Peek-a-Boo Toodles" and made by the American Character Co. Made from 1956. Little one in a Newborn Thumbelina made by Ideal Doll Co. Cloth and vinyl and marked: 1967/Ideal, in circle, TT-8-H-108, on head. Courtesy Phyllis Teague. $50.00.

AMERICAN CHARACTER
ARRANBEE

19'' Butterball. All vinyl Sleep eyes/lashes. Upper lip protrudes. Marks: 1961 American Doll & Toy Co. An original dress. Courtesy Doris Richardson. $45.00.

18'' Toodle-Loo with painted brown eyes and rooted hair. Made of "Magic Foam" plastic with vinyl head. Marks; American Doll & Toy Co. 1961. Courtesy Doris Richardson. $65.00.

17'' Nancy. Lovely quality rayon taffeta in pink with nosegays of tea roses, blue flowers and green leaves. Dress is completely bound around bottom in a scolloped effect, and she holds a matching umbrella and dress is tied to wrists to hold up. Bodice is lace with pink satin ribbon, and neck is trimmed in lace, matching hat. Heavy eye shadow, open mouth/4 teeth and blue sleep eyes. 1938. Made by Arranbee Doll Co., "Nancy" was in competition to the Princess Elizabeth dolls. Courtesy June Schultz.

12''	$ 45.00 Mint	$25.00 Crazed, original
17''	$ 75.00 Mint	$35.00 Crazed, original
19''	$ 95.00 Mint	$45.00 Crazed, original
23''	$125.00 Mint	$55.00 Crazed, original

ARRANBEE

Arranbee NANCY ALL composition - all original 17''
Yellow/green print organdy dress. White straw hat
with green trim and large yellow flower. Brown sleep
eyes open mouth four teeth. Marks: Nancy on head.
Courtesy Sue Austin. $75.00.

21'' Sonja Henie by Arranbee Doll Co. and marked R
& B, on head. All composition with mohair wig and
sleep eyes/lashes. (Brown). Red felt hat, coat and
dress. White high top ice skates. Closed mouth. All
original. Courtesy Jackie Barker. $90.00.

18'' Sonja Henie Skater. All composition, sleep eyes
and closed mouth. All original outfit. White with red
trim. Made by Arranbee Doll Co. Some will be marked
with an ''R & B'', on head. Courtesy Mary Williams.
$80.00.

176

ARRANBEE

11'' W.W. 2 Nurse. Composition with cloth body (same as the Debu-teen dolls). Sleep eyes and closed mouth. Heavy satin gown. Almost white, glued on wig. Clothes are stapled on. Made by Arranbee. Courtesy Dorothy Peters. $45.00.

Shows underclothes and legs of 11'' R & B doll. Courtesy Dorothy Peters.

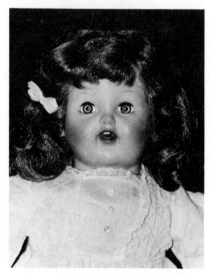

19'' Dream Baby. Oil cloth, stuffed body with vinyl head and limbs. Sleep blue eyes/lashes. Open/closed mouth with two upper teeth. Painted lashes under eyes only. Glued on saran wig over molded hair. Her pink dress may be original. Marks: Arranbee, on head. 1954. Courtesy Bessie Carson. $30.00.

23'' Angel Face. By Arranbee Doll Co. Cloth body with vinyl head, blue sleep eyes/lashes. Vinyl arms and legs that are ''little girl'' with all fingers separated. White glued on wig. 1954. Courtesy Kimport Dolls. 16'' - $22.00, 23'' - $28.00.

ARRANBEE
BABY BERRY
BUBBLES

14'' Late Nancy Lee Bride. All hard plastic with jointed knees, walker and head does not turn. Saran glued on wig. Mark: R & B (Arranbee), on head. Courtesy June Schultz. Late - $40.00, Nanette type -$55.00.

24'' Emmett Kelly dressed as ''Willie the Clown''. Vinyl head with set in eyes, rooted red hair, stuffed cloth body and original clothes tagged: Exclusive Lincence/Baby Berry Toy NYC. Ca. 1958. Courtesy Ann Wencel. $85.00.

17'' Charlie Chaplin. Molded vinyl head with painted features. Hat, collar & tie molded onto head. Molded hands and shoes. Body is stuffed cloth. Wooden cane. Black felt jacket, gray cotton pants, print cotton vest. Top of original box. Marks: Bubbles Inc./1972, on back of head. Courtesy Allan Tay. $45.00.

178

CAMEO

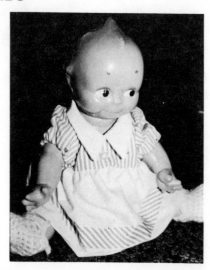

KEWPIES

All bisque: Made by many German doll makers, with most from the Kestner factory. The "Kewpie" designer and copyright owner was Rose O'Neill. There were a great many "Kewpie" copies, so a collector must study and know "Kewpies" before paying high prices.

4''-5'' Standing, one piece body, head and legs. Blue wings, jointed shoulders only, painted eyes to side - $85.00. 7''-8'' Description same as above - $125.00 - $165.00. 6'' Same description except jointed at shoulders and hips - $450.00.

Action Kewpies: All molded in one piece (figurine) Any Kewpie in action form such as, Thinker, Traveller with suitcase, playing instrument, Soldiers, with cat, Policeman, molded on clothes, with gun, etc. - $250.00 - $450.00.

Action Kewpies, Special: All molded in one piece. With dog - $550.00. Kewpiedoodle dog along - $250.00. Soldier/vase - $475.00. Sitting at table, with tea service -$1,200.00. With bee on bottom of foot - $375.00. On sled - $575.00. With Teddy Bear - $400.00.

Bisque heads: Cloth body, bisque arms, sew holes to shoulder head with attach head. Painted eyes. 7'' - $495.00. 9'' - $650.00. 12'' - $1,000.00. Cloth body with flanged neck bisque head, bisque hands, Glass eyes 9'' - $2,800.00. 12'' - $3,600.00. 15'' - $4,800.00. 12'' Bisque socket head on five piece composition body, glass eyes -$3,600.00. 15'' Bisque socket head on composition body with extra joints at elbows and knees, glass eyes - $4,000.00.

Celluloid Kewpies: Molded one piece body, head and legs. Only shoulders are jointed. Made in Deuben, Germany by Karl Standfuss. 2½'' - $25.00. 3½'' - $25.00. 5½'' -$45.00. 8'' - $65.00. 10'' - $75.00. 12'' - $85.00.

Composition Kewpies: One piece body, head and legs. Jointed at shoulders only. 12'' -$75.00 jointed at hips and shoulders. 12'' - $95.00.

CAMEO

Cuddlers, all cloth Kewpies: Mask face with painted features, stuffed cloth body and limbs. Made by the Richard G. Kreuger Co. of New York. If label still intact, it will be sewn on side seam: 12'' - $65.00, 14'' - $85.00.

Hard plastic Kewpies: All hard plastic with one piece body, head and legs. Jointed at shoulders only. 9'' - $45.00. All hard plastic, jointed at hips and shoulders. 9'' -$65.00. 12'' - $95.00. 15'' - $125.00.

Vinyl Kewpies: All vinyl with one piece body, head and legs. Jointed shoulders only. 7'' - $10.00. 12'' - $20.00. All vinyl, jointed at shoulders and hips. 8'' - $25.00. 9'' - $30.00. 12'' - $45.00.

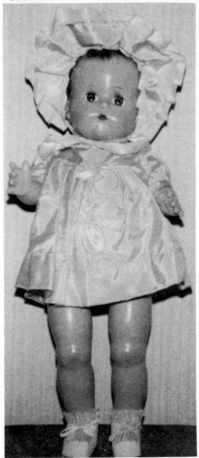

20½'' Sally Lou. All composition, all original. No marks on doll or clothes. Box: No. 120A "Sally Lou"/Original Jos Kallus, when he was with the Mutual Doll Co. (Cameo) Molded hair, brown sleep eyes. The dress and bonnet are peach taffeta. Courtesy June Schultz. $60.00.

15'' Miss Peep made by Cameo Doll Co. All vinyl with pin jointed hips and shoulders. Molded hair and set blue eyes. Cryer in arms. Marks: Cameo, on head and body. This doll was made for a great many years, from 1956, so the date is almost impossible to tell. Courtesy Phyllis Teague. $20.00.

CAMEO
CLOTH

12" Betty Boop. All composition and wood with extra joints in arms and legs. Molded black hair, painted features, with eyes to side. Dress is molded on and has heart shaped label: "Betty Boop"/Des. & Copryright/ by Fleiscker/Studios. Courtesy Jackie Barker. 12" Mint - $375.00. 12" Crazed and Flaking - $200.00. 12" Crazed, crack, paint gone - $75.00.

The Betty Boop doll was molded, designed and copyrighted by Joseph L. Kallus (Cameo Doll Co.) The Fleischer Studios copyrighted the animated cartoons.

24" Oil painted mask face nailed on to composition head that is painted yellow. Jointed at neck only. Flesh colored cotton stuffed muslin torso, and limbs. Arms have stitched thumb and fingers. Molded shoes, flat footed (Cardboard inside). Intaglio brown eyes with inset lashes and blonde Shirley Temple mohair wig. Redressed. Ca. early 1930's. Same construction as Madame Hendren used on her "Next to Nature" dolls, but this one is unmarked. 9" long, 8" high grey felt straw stuffed elephant on wheels. Shoe button eyes, red felt circus blanket, rayon covered straw tusks, bronze painted iron wheels marked "Schuco Patent". Turn tail and head moves. Pull toy ca: 1930 or earlier. Courtesy Margaret Mandel. Doll - $125.00 up, Toy -$75.00 up.

Close up of the unmarked mask face over composition doll.

12'' Lady who looks very much like "Wally" Simpson who married the ex-King of England in the 1930's. All cloth with oil painted features. Dressed in velvet and lace. Marks: G. McAlpin, Gilmer, Texas, is printed on underclothes. $85.00.

CLOTH

23'' Cloth doll with rayon, straw filled, body. Painted silk face. Original clothes. No marks: Ca. 1935. Courtesy Penny Pendlebury. $25.00.

20'' All cloth with buckram face mask that has oil painted features. All original. Mohair wig stitched on. All fingers separate. No marks. $65.00.

15'' All stuffed oilcloth doll with painted features. All clothes are sewn on. No marks. $12.00.

CLOTH

14'' Painted mask buckrum face, blonde mohair wig cap, unjointed oil cloth body, arms (curved to hold a pail that is missing), painted blue eyes, original blue cotton dress, white organdy apron and Dutch cap. Original shoes and socks Tag: Krueger. 1940's. 13'' All straw stuffed Donkey sitting. Early plush head, unjointed cloth body with sewn on velvet feet and hands, original glass eyes and original orange felt overalls, green felt jacket with felt trim. Very rare. 1910 or earlier. Courtesy Margaret Mandel. Doll - $45.00, Toy - $75.00.

20'' Mollye International doll that is all cloth with buckram mask face with painted features. Red cotton skirt trimmed in gold rayon ribbon, green velvet shoes sewn on, black mantilla with pink flowers. Unmarked. Shown with her is a 9'' Steiff bear on cast iron wheels. Has original PEWTER ear clip with "ff" underscored, indicating he was made before 1920. "Steiff" imprinted on leather collar. Made of worsted material, not mohair. Straw stuffed. Courtesy Margaret Mandel. Doll - $85.00, Bear - $200.00

CLOTH

25'' All cloth that is cotton stuffed with unjointed limbs, but constructed so that neck raises and lowers in cloth socket. Painted mask face, blue eyes, yellow yarn hair, detachable blue skirt only with sewn on blouse and shoes. Early 1940's. These dolls also came with straps across feet to attach to child's feet and become a dancing partner. Bear on left: 12'' gold long mohair, fully jointed and cotton stuffed. Bristle mohair nose, original nose embroidered with yarn not thread or floss, orange tin (decal) eyes. A very rare bear. Ca. 1930. Bear on right: 17'' early and rare bear, straw filled, fully jointed and made from brown worsted wool. Original shoe button eyes, long curved arms, long nose and original canvas pads. Before 1910. Doll - $35.00, Left - $50.00 up, Right - $90.00 up.

14'' Cloth dolls Jack and Jill. Mask faces with painted blue eyes to the side. Body and limbs are flesh nylon type material, clothes are blue felt with white organdy tops. They have saran wigs. Maker is unknown, but an educated guess would be Madame Hendron. Courtesy Jackie Barker. (Dolls were given to her for Christmas 1946). $50.00

CLOTH

20'' Danial Boone. Pressed plastic coated face mask. Remainder is stuffed plush material. Sewn feet accents. Pin reads: UAW-CIO/Jan.-Feb. 1956. No marks or tags. $25.00.

16'' Black cloth doll, button jointed. Yarn hair and has natural fiber skirt and ankles. Embroidered features, felt mouth, and replaced ear and nose rings. Nicely made and appears to be from about the 1950's. Courtesy Nancy Lucas. $20.00.

16'' Alice in Wonderland. All cloth with painted features and yarn hair. All original. Tag: Childhood Classics, NY, NY. Courtesy Betty Tait. $45.00.

CLOTH

15" "Jimmy Carter". All lithographed cloth head, check cloth torso and arms, denuim lower body and legs. Stuffed "bean bag" type. Marks: Kasia '77, printed on neck. Tag: Another Friendly Feeling. $20.00.

12" Tubby of the Little Lulu comics. All cloth with yellow yarn hair, blue and white beany cap on back of head. Courtesy Kimport Dolls. $40.00.

21" Amy Carter. All cloth with felt glasses and yarn hair. Tag: An original/Tom McPortland's/by Lim Co. L.A./Pat. Pending/Copyright 1978. $22.00.

CLOTH

7'' Ben Franklin. All cloth lithographed doll. Made by Hallmark for the Bi-Centennial. Courtesy Nancy Lucas. $25.00.

7'' Betsy Ross Bi-Centennial doll made by Hallmark and so tagged. All cloth lithographed. A very difficult doll to find. Courtesy Nancy Lucas. $50.00.

7'' George Washington. All lithograph cloth and made by and tagged: Hallmark. One of the Bi-Centennial dolls. Courtesy Nancy Lucas. $25.00.

7'' Martha Washington. Hallmarks Bi-Centennial all cloth, lithographed doll. This seems to be the hardest one in the series to obtain. Courtesy Nancy Lucas. $25.00.

CLOTH
COLORFORMS
COMMONWEALTH

27'' This is one of the re-issue (new) and available Lenci dolls. The Lenci Company has maintained their superior quality in these re-issue dolls. Courtesy Mary Williams. $250.00-$375.00.

6½'' Commander Comet. Man from Venus. All flexable vinyl with detachable plastic wings. Marked: Made in Hong Kong. Made by Colorforms and there were seven in the set. 1967. Gift from the Bougious family. $8.00.

15'' Superman. Felt and plush body and limbs. Vinyl portrait head with molded hair and painted features. Marks: Nat. Per. Pub. Com. Toy., around the base of the neck. Tag: Superman/National Periodical/Publications, Inc. 1966, on one side. Other side: Commonwealth/Toy & Novelty Co. Inc. $35.00.

COSMOPOLITION
DAKIN, R.

8" Ginger. All hard plastic with sleep eyes and closed mouth. Walker, head turns. Original ballerina outfit. Doll is not marked. Made by Cosmopolition. All hard plastic - $12.00, Vinyl head - $10.00.

24" Lucy Mae. All cloth with wide bottom so she will sit down. Orange body and attached panties with pocket. Pink arms and head. Felt features. Troll-type hair. Black and white stripe legs with attached green felt shoes. Green removable dress. One shoe ties and other buckles. Tag: Lucy Mae/R. Dakin & Company. 1967. $18.00.

5" Smokey the Bear. Put out by AIM Toothpaste. Tagged #3535 R. Dakin & Co. San Francisco. Prod. of Hong Kong. Front tag: Official Licensee-Cooperative Forest Fire Preventive Program. He has "Prevent Forest Fires" on shovel. "Smokey" on belt and hat. "Smokey Bear" cloth tag on pants, plus the R. Dakin information. Plastic with cloth pants. Courtesy Renie Culp. $10.00.

DELUXE TOPPER
DISNEY, WALT

Dawn's "Flower Fantasy". There are five different. This dress had a red top with white/gold collar & skirt. Marks: 804/K11A. Flower pot is yellow. One in a blue pot was marked: 685/N11A. $8.00.

11½" Pinocchio. All composition, jointed neck, shoulders and hips. Molded hair and painted eyes. Original clothes. White shirt/red pants with yellow buttons and hat. White gloves are molded on Marks: Pinocchio Disney Prod., on head. Disney Prod Made in USA/Crown Toy Co., on body. Courtesy A.P. Miller Collection. $85.00.

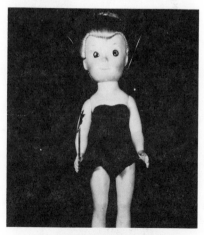

18" Mickey Mouse that is all bendable, poreous vinyl. Marks: Bend-A-Twist/Multi Plastic/Fort Lauderdale, Fla./Walt Disney Production. Courtesy Kimport Dolls. $65.00.

12" Tinkerbell. All soft vinyl with rooted blonde hair. Set blue eyes, closed mouth and open hands facing body. Plastic wings and felt clothes. Marks: Walt Disney Prod. on bottom of right foot. Made by Sayco. 1950. $15.00.

DOLL ARTIST

Doll Artist dolls by Emma Clear: Emma Clear was owner and operator of the Humpty Dumpty Doll Hospital in Redondo Beach, Calif. During the 1940's she reproduced the most exquisite China and Parian dolls available. Even to this day no other ''artist'' has been able to match her work and skill. Emma Clear died in 1951 and her friend, student bought out the Humpty Dumpty Doll Hospital and continued making the finest reproductions. Her name was Mrs. Lillian Smith. Emma Clear's own dolls will be marked with ''Clear'' in script and most often a date (for example '49) will be found inside the ''C''. If the name Smith is also present, then the Clear mold was painted by Lillian Smith. Emma Clear also commissioned artist Martha Oathout Ayres to do some originals for her, such as the George and Martha Washingtons.

Emma Clear Dolls: Parians with elaborate hairdos, combs, scarfs, bonnets, braids, and painted eyes, 18'' - $250.00. Parians, same as above but with glass eyes, 18'' -$350.00. Chinas, ladies, 18'' - $200.00, 23'' - $300.00. Men, 18'' - $250.00, 23'' - $350.00. George and Martha Washington, 20'' - $300.00, set - $700.00.

21'' Rare hair style china made by Emma Clear. The old dolls like this one almost always had a pink luster in glaze finish and this one does not. Courtesy Kimport Dolls. $225.00.

DOLL ARTIST

28'' Bisque head on old German, fully jointed, composition and wood body. Closed mouth with molded porcelain teeth, set glass eyes/lashes. Marks: T.M. Artist is unknown. $325.00.

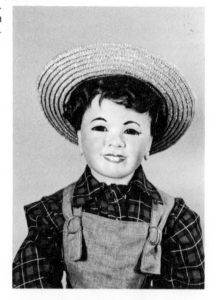

20'' Original cloth doll named ''Felicia'' designed and made in 1979 by Phyllis Teague. Unknown prices.

A ''Pennydoll'' wax reproduction of a 1923 By-Lo Baby made and courtesy of Penny Pendlebury. $185.00.

EEGEE
EFFANBEE

Eegee Dolls: 17'' Gigi Perreaux. Hard plastic with vinyl head. Brown sleep eyes, open/closed mouth with painted teeth. (referance: Modern Collector's Dolls-1, page 74) Marks: E.G., on head - $150.00.

16'' Flowerkins. Large "googly" eyes. Marks: F2/Eegee, on head - $45.00.

20'' Ballerina. Hard plastic with jointed knees and ankles, vinyl arms and head. Marks: 14R, on head - $22.00.

12'' Baby Luv. Cloth and vinyl with large painted eyes. Marks: 14BT/Eegee Co. -$35.00.

17'' Miss Sunbeam. Plastic and vinyl with open/closed smiling mouth, painted teeth and deep cheek dimples. Marks: Eegee, on head - $25.00.

14'' Granny (from Beverly Hillbillies) Plastic and vinyl with "old lady" modeling. Grey rooted hair and brows. Painted or sleep eyes. Marks: Eegee/3, on head - $75.00.

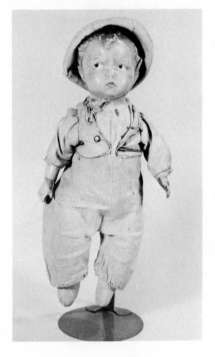

10½'' Lil' Susan. Hard plastic body and limbs with jointed knees, vinyl head with rooted hair, sleep eyes and closed mouth. Original cowgirl outfit. Packaged single and in trunks with wardrobes. 1955-1957. Made by Eegee. Doll alone - $12.00, In trunk with wardrobe: $32.00.

15'' Grumpy. Composition head and lower arms. Rest is tightly stuffed cloth. Toddler legs. Deeply molded hair, painted features with intaglio eyes. Pouty. Original two piece outfit. No marks. Grumpy was a successful doll made by Effanbee for many years. (1912-1939) Courtesy Kimport Dolls. $100.00.

15'' First Patsy. Composition shoulder head (does not swivel), cloth body and composition limbs. Open mouth, dimples and molded hair under original red mohair wig. Sleep brown eyes. Original blue one piece suit. Marks: Effanbee/Patsy, on back of shoulder. These first Patsys were the Baby Dainty molds. 1924. Courtesy Ruth Fisher. $100.00.

EFFANBEE

14'' Patsy. All composition, original wig and clothes. Shown with Butterick pattern for Patsy clothes. Has original pin and wrist tag. Courtesy Marge Meisinger. $135.00.

6'' Wee Patsy, mint & original - $100.00. Light craze, played with, original -$60.00. Craze, not original clothes - $25.00.

8'' Patsy Babyete, mint & original - $95.00. Light craze, played with, original -$45.00. Craze, not original clothes - $20.00.

9'' Patsyette, mint and original - $85.00. Light craze, played with, original - $40.00. Craze, not original clothes - $20.00.

10'' Patsy Baby, mint and original - $85.00. Light craze, played with, original -$40.00. Craze, not original clothes - $20.00.

11'' Patsy Jr., mint and original - $90.00. Light craze, played with, original -$45.00. Craze, not original clothes - $25.00.

14'' Patsy, mint and original - $135.00. Light craze, played with, original - $75.00. Craze, not original clothes - $30.00.

14'' Patricia, mint and original - $145.00. Light craze, played with, original -$75.00. Craze, not original - $30.00.

16'' Patsy Joan, mint and original - $165.00. Light craze, played with, original -$85.00. Craze, not original clothes - $40.00.

19'' Patsy Ann, mint and original - $185.00. Light craze, played with, original -$90.00. Craze, not original clothes - $45.00.

22'' Patsy Lou, mint and original - $195.00. Light craze, played with, original -$95.00. Craze, not original clothes - $45.00.

26'' Patsy Ruth, mint and original - $265.00. Light craze, played with, original -$100.00. Craze, not original clothes - $50.00.

30'' Patsy Mae, mint and original - $300.00. Light craze, played with, original -$125.00. Craze, not original clothes - $65.00.

EFFANBEE

9'' Patsyette. All composition with molded hair and painted eyes. Courtesy Diane Hoffman. Mint and original - $85.00, mint and nude - $55.00.

8'' Patsy Babyette by Effanbee. All compostion with brown sleep eyes, caracul fur wig and closed mouth. Dress may be original. Marked Patsy Babyette/Effanbee on back. Also came with molded hair. 1927. Courtesy Pam Ortman. $95.00.

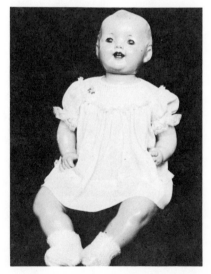

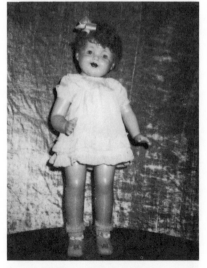

20'' Lovums by Effanbee. Composition shoulder plate and head, arms and legs and rest cloth. Clothes are not original. Marks: Effanbee/Lovums/Pat/#1,283,558. 1928. Courtesy Pam Ortman. 16'' - $85.00, 20'' -$95.00.

22'' Lovums, Girl Version. All composition with open mouth with two upper and two lower teeth. Red caracul/lambs wool wig over molded hair. Sleep eyes. Original with pink teddies and dress tagged: Effanbee/Durable Dolls. 1928. Courtesy Mildred Hightower. Photo by Cindy Hightower. 22'' -$115.00.

EFFANBEE

15" Patricia. All composition and original. The human hair wig is tosca and set in curls. The sleep eyes are brown and the dress is aqua with sewn on flowers. The doll is marked Effanbee Patricia. 1932. Courtesy Gloyra Woods. $145.00.

15" Patricia. All composition and original. Dress is multi-colored with green rick-rack. Wig is orange-red 9" Patsyette. All composition with molded hair and painted eyes. Courtesy Diane Hoffman. Mint and original - $85.00, mint and nude - $55.00.

19" Patsy Ann. All composition with bent right arm. Original clothes. Shown with book by Mona Reed King, published in 1935 by Rand McNally. White mohair Patsy chow dog. 8½" high. Dog is straw stuffed. Both doll and dog by Effanbee Doll Co. Courtesy Margaret Mandel. $185.00, Dog - $25.00.

198

EFFANBEE

17'' Barbara Lou/Ice Queen (designed by Dewees Cochran). All composition with sleep eyes, open mouth and feathered brows. Has chunky child type body with well formed child's legs and arms, with the typical "Anne Shirley" style open hands. (To take gloves). Original clothes and human hair wig. This doll used for "Ice Queen" was very elaborately dressed in Ice Skating outfit. Made by Effanbee. 1938. Courtesy Hightower. 17'' Barbara Lou - $125.00. 17'' Ice Queen - $150.00.

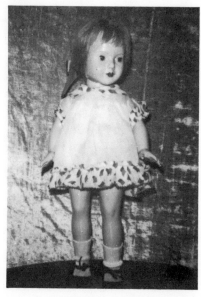

14'' One of the Baby Bright Eyes series. (Boy version is Tommy Bangs and has wig). Cloth body with composition head and limbs. Head attached to body with wooden plug. Brown sleep eyes/lashes. Molded hair under wig. Original pink and white dress. Marks: Effanbee, on head. 1940. Courtesy Kimport Dolls. $65.00.

12'' Effanbee Portrait Doll dressed in majorette outfit that is original. All composition with sleep eyes, closed "rosebud" mouth, blonde wig. Doll is unmarked. 1940. Courtesy Jackie Barker. $65.00.

EFFANBEE

24'' Honey Ann. Hard plastic walker, blue sleep eyes, blonde saran wig, original pink, purple and white rayon dress. Replaced shoes and socks. 1952-54. Made by Effanbee. 12'' Celluloid type Kathe Kruse baby, painted brown eyes, rosebud mouth. Marks: 31, on back. Some 15 years ago the Kathe Kruse factory gave other doll factories license to make dolls under the Kruse name. Courtesy Margaret Mandel. $95.00.

14'' Honey Majorette. All hard plastic with sleep eyes and closed mouth. Open hands with all fingers extended. Glued on floss type hair in tight cluster curls. Mark: Effanbee, on head and body. The Honey line ran from 1949 through 1955. 14'' - $60.00, 18'' -$75.00, 21'' - $95.00.

10'' Mickey the Clown. All vinyl with white arms and head. Molded, black hair and painted features. Original, minus hat and shoes. Marks: Mickey/Effanbee, on head. 1956. $15.00

200

EFFANBEE

10½'' Mickey Ball Player. All good quality vinyl with molded hair and hat. Painted blue eyes to the side. Freckles and closed smiling mouth. Marks: Effanbee, on head. 1956. $15.00.

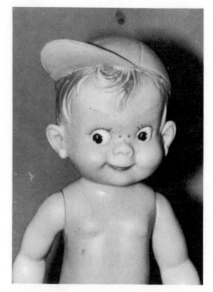

18'' Lawerence Welk's Champagne Lady. 1957. Rigid plastic body with hard plastic legs that have jointed knees and ankles. Vinyl arms and head. Sleep blue eyes, pierced ears and high heel feet. White satin half slip with green trim and net ''can can'' half slip. Green satin dress, rhinestone bab and silver slippers. Elbow gloves and rhinestone solataire. Marks: Effanbee, on head. Courtesy Marjorie Uhl. $85.00.

30'' Mary Jane. Plastic and vinyl with rooted hair, sleep eyes and closed mouth. 1960. Made by Effanbee Doll Co. Some are marked, and others are not. Courtesy Phyllis Teague. $100.00.

EFFANBEE

24'' Baby Thumkin by Effanbee. Cloth with vinyl head and limbs. Large sleep eyes, rooted hair and open/closed mouth. Original. Marks: Effanbee/1965. Courtesy Doris Richardson. 18'' - $30.00, 24'' - $45.00.

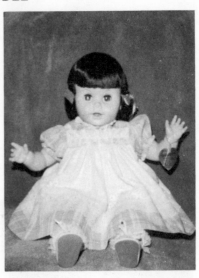

26'' Precious Baby. Cloth and vinyl head and limbs. Rooted dark brown hair, sleep blue eyes and open/closed mouth. Original. Marks: Effanbee/1967, on head. Courtesy Doris Richardson. $40.00.

12'' Butterball. All vinyl with molded hair, sleep eyes/lashes and a very chubby baby. Original, including bottle and blanket. Marks: Effanbee/1969/6569, on head. Courtesy Phyllis Teague. $16.00.

18'' Susie Sunshine. Plastic with vinyl arms. Sleep blue eyes/lashes. Freckles. Left hand 2nd and 3rd fingers molded together. Original pink check gown with white organdy pinafore. 1972. $45.00.

EFFANBEE
FLAGG

These are the Effanbee Dolls made only for Disneyland and Disneyworld. Left to right: Sleeping Beauty, Alice in Wonderland, Cinderella and Snow White. In front is the Mary Poppins set by Horsman dolls. Courtesy Mary Williams. Effanbee Doll - currently available, Mary Poppins - $20.00, Children - $25.00.

6'' Flagg doll Can Can dancer in bright yellow dress with shocking pink trim. Courtesy Donnie Durant. $10.00.

6'' Flagg doll that is all posable vinyl. Geisha Girl in pastel print gown. Courtesy Donnie Durant. $10.00.

FOREIGN

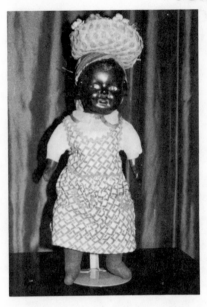

15" Jamaica. Cloth body with cloth legs. Composition arms and head with molded black hair and painted eyes to the side. Closed smiling mouth. Marks: A Reliable Doll/Made in Canada. Carries a basket of fruit on head. Courtesy A.P. Miller Collection. $22.00.

15" .Cloth with composition head and limbs. Blue sleep eyes, closed mouth and molded hair. All original. Bought in 1942, and made by the Reliable Doll Co. of Canada. Courtesy Jil Ashmore. $35.00.

22" French celluloid with glass, flirty eyes. Doll is completely celluloid, and jointed at neck, hips and shoulders. Open mouth. Dressed from the French Province of Pont-Aven (Brittany). Doll was given to the owner in 1945. Courtesy Carole Nori. $125.00.

FOREIGN

18" Bella. All plastic with brown sleep eyes that follow you. Rooted hair, pierced ears and has a cryer in back. Marks: Bella/Made in France, on back. All original, except shoes. Pin on dress: Bella. Courtesy Nancy Lucas. $40.00.

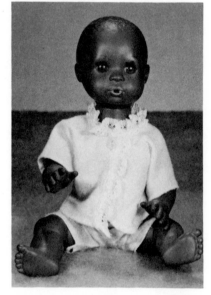

10½" All vinyl. Black baby made in Germany. He is marked with a turtle in a diamond, on head and body with a 30 under it, on body. Clothes appear to be original. Brown sleep eyes, black molded hair. Made by Rheinische Gumme und Celluloid Fabrik Co. Ca. 1960's. Courtesy Nancy Lucas. $35.00.

13½" All celluloid, with one piece body and head. Blue painted eyes and molded hair. All original. Marks: (curved) DukkeskoFabriken/Mitri, on bottom of shoes. 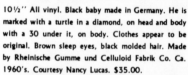 , on back. Courtesy Nancy Lucas. $30.00.

SK
KØGE

205

12'' All vinyl doll with rooted hair and sleep blue eyes/lashes. Marks: Gotz/West Germany. Courtesy Renie Culp. $22.00.

19'' . Thin rigid plastic with flirty eyes and in original clothes. Purchased in Germany in 1958. Doll is not marked, but tag reads: Cell-Kopt/Kammbar/Onduberban/Mama, other side A crown/Seit E.K. Courtesy Jil Ashmore. $100.00.

7 ¼'' Lilli of Germany. The most sought after doll, to Barbie collectors, after the #1 Barbie doll. All rigid plastic with holes in feet for stand. Doll is unmarked. All original. Courtesy Bernice Lieb. 7 ¼'' Lilli -$100.00 up, 11'' Lilli - $150.00 up.

A #2 Brunette Barbie is shown with the 7 ¼'' version of the standard 11½'' Lilli from Germany. Original clothes on both dolls. Courtesy Bernice Lieb. #2 Barbie - $75.00 up.

FOREIGN

14'' (seated) Hungarian Nursing mother and baby. Beautifully hand made and embroidered clothes. Bought in 1972 in Budapest. This doll recieved a 1st place ribbon at the UFDC, Portland, Oregon 1978 Regional Convention. Courtesy Jil Ashmore. $75.00.

24'' Italian Walking doll. Heavy body that feels like metal, has cryer box in stomach, large sleep blue eyes, glued on wig and fingernails are painted deep red. Has rollers on bottom of feet to walk, but no apparent power source. Marks: Brevettato, on back. Courtesy $50.00.

Shows the rollers on the bottom of the feet of the 24'' Italian doll. There are no key winds, or batteries, so how the doll operated is a mystery. Courtesy

FOREIGN

8'' Tiny Furga. All vinyl with sleep eyes and rooted hair. All original. Marks: L. Furga 1977, on head. Made in Hong Kong/L. Furga 1977, on back. Courtesy Renie Culp. $25.00.

4'' Characters that are made of all wood and were made in Japan. Courtesy Renie Culp. $9.00 each.

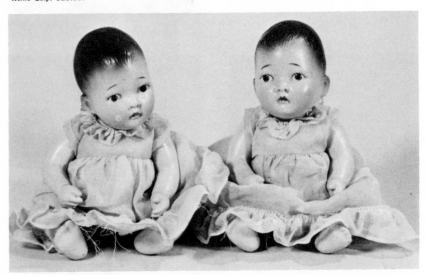

7½'' Two from set of Quints. All composition, bent leg babies. Painted blue eyes, right hand molded with fingers cupped. Jointed at neck, shoulders and hips. Organza type, ruffled dresses with cotton slips. Modeled and painted hair. ''Japan'' is stamped on dolls and on clothes. Above average quality for Japanese compostion. Ca. 1935-36. Courtesy Kimport Dolls. $30.00 each.

FOREIGN
FUN WORLD

12" All wood oriental figure. Lathe carved. Hand painted decoration. Marks: Oriental symbols on base. Date unknown, but most likely 1970-1975. $4.00.

15" Stockinette doll made in Korea. Ca. 1974. Since early 1975 the stores seem to be located with these dolls, in a great many different costumes, it would be impossible to keep up with them. Each year see's more and more of these imports. Made at the So Yea Doll Institute in Seoul, Korea. Courtesy Phyllis Houston.

8" Let's Pretend. Plastic with vinyl head. Rooted hair and painted blue eyes. Marks: Hong Kong on head. A more reasonably priced doll, but masks and outfits are excellent quality. There are two sets: Indian/Monster and Clown/Granny. Made by Fun World. Courtesy Marie Ernst. $6.00.

GAY BOB

12'' Gay Bob. Plastic and vinyl full jointed action figure. Flocked hair, painted blue eyes, left ear is pierced. Heavily sexed (adult). Marks: /A looked like ''Barter'' Toy/Hong Kong/Div. of Harvey Rosenberg/Inc. 1977. Box: Style #GB101/ Distributed by Gay Bob Trading Co. Inc. Box 461, N.Y., N.Y. 10024. $16.00.

Gay Bob is supposed to have other dolls join him on the shelves and they are to be: Nervous Nellie, Anxious Abbey, Liberated Fran, Fashionable Sisters, Straight Steve, Heavy Harry, Fat Pat, Marty Macho, Executive Eddie. They are to be presented in various costumes and props.

GERBER BABY
HALL
HOBY

10½'' Black Gerber Baby of 1972. Head marked: The Gerber Baby/Gerber Prod. Co./1972. Pajama's are tagged: Gerber. Made in British Crown Colony of Hong Kong. Painted brown eyes, fully jointed and all vinyl. Same as the White version of 1972. Courtesy Nancy Lucas. 10½'' white - $20.00, 10½'' black -$45.00.

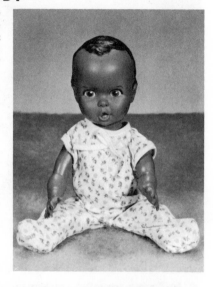

8'' Dennis, the Menace. This comic strip character is plastic and vinyl with one piece body. Painted features and clothes. Marks: The Hall Synd. Inc., on right foot. 1959, on left foot. Courtesy Penny Pendlebury. $20.00.

21½'' Hody's restuarant clown. Cloth with vinyl head. Vinyl hat molded on. The hands and feet are felt. Marks: Hody's, on hat. During the 1950's there was a Hody restuarant in Long Beach, California, which burned down in the 1960's. Courtesy Arlene Mitgel. $45.00.

211

HORSMAN

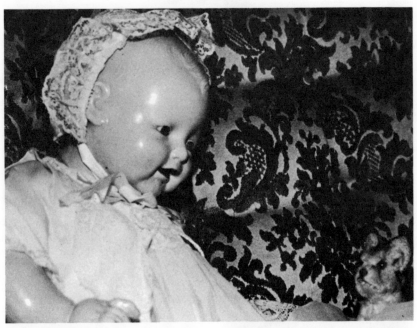

22" Baby Dimples by Horsman Dolls. Composition and cloth with open mouth and sleep tin eyes. Not original. Marks: E.I.H. Co. Inc. Courtesy Mary Sweeney. $85.00.

15" Betty Jo. All composition with mohair wig, sleep eyes. Slight "look" of a Shirley Temple doll. The clothes are original and designed and made by Mollye Goldman, under contract with the Horsman Doll Co. 1935. Courtesy Sharon Ivy. $65.00.

12" Chubby Toddler. All composition with tin sleep eyes. Mohair braided wig. Marks: Horsman Doll Co., on head. Courtesy Pam Ortman. $35.00.

HORSMAN

Close up of Horsman Doll of 1938.

18'' Cynthia. All composition twins with blue tin sleep eyes, yellow mohair wigs in braids pigtails. Original rose net formals with blue ribbon trim, bent right arms. 1938. Clothes designed by Mollye. Courtesy Margaret Mandel. $85.00.

12'' Campbell Kid. All composition with painted eyes and molded hair. Made by Horsman dolls in 1948. $75.00.

18'' Chubby faced composition baby with cloth body. Sleep eyes and open/closed mouth. Molded hair. This baby was also made with composition body. Marks: E.I.H., on head. Dates from early 1930's through 1939. Courtesy Diane Hoffman.

HORSMAN

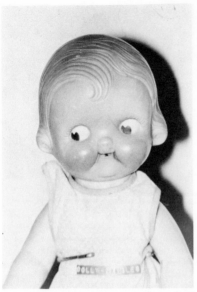

12' Campbell Kid or Dolly Dingle. Unique in that it is all very early vinyl that is stuffed. Jointed at hips and shoulders with disks inside body. No marks. Most likely is a 1949 or 1950 doll made by Horsman, as they made the one like this, in composition, in 1948. Courtesy Kimport Dolls. $45.00.

27'' Cindy Strutter. 1954. Hard plastic walker, head turns and is not jointed at knees. All fingers separate and arms only rotate to near straight up position. Vinyl head with sleep blue eyes/lashes and painted lashes below only, thinly molded upper lids. Rooted saran hair. Original grey/blue ball gown with shoulder straps crossing in back and snapped. Marks: None, although some are marked Horsman/c-27, on head. $85.00.

18'' Cindy Ruth by Horsman Doll Co. Came in red card board trunk with 2 extra dresses, lime green slacks. Closed smile mouth, large blue sleep eyes/lashes and rooted hair. The doll is all vinyl of excellent quality. Marks: Horsman, on head. 1960. Was used as "Grown up Miss" - 1961 and "Sub Teen-Beauty" in 1962. Courtesy Helena Street. $35.00.

HORSMAN

26" Ruth's Sister of 1960. Plastic with vinyl head and arms. Rooted hair, sleep eyes and open/closed mouth. Walker when lead by hand. Marks: T-27/Horsman, on head. 25-6/AE, on back. Original. Courtesy Phyllis Teague. $35.00.

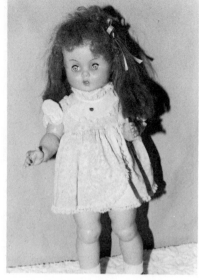

16" Excellent quality all vinyl with sleep vivid blue eyes/lashes. Open mouth/nurser. Three fingers curled on left hand. Fourth finger deeply curled and third slightly curled on right hand. Toes are all slightly curled. Marks: Horsman Doll, Inc./ 1972, on head. Horsman Doll, Inc./13 11 H, on back. 20, upper & 16 HH, lower legs (other leg has 13HH). 1 H 4/26 under one arm and 1 H 4/23 under other arm. $15.00.

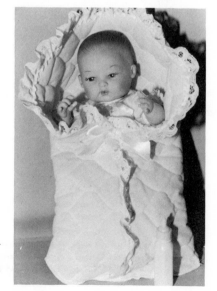

14" 1977 version of the Bye-lo baby. Molded hair and painted eyes. Open mouth/nurser and all vinyl. Marks: Horsman Dolls, Inc. 13-1977, on head and body. Courtesy Phyllis Teague. Still Available.

HOYER, MARY

14'' Both are all original Mary Hoyer dolls that are all hard plastic. Sleep eyes and glued on wigs. 2nd and 3rd fingers are molded together and slightly curled. Both are marked Original/Mary Hoyer/Doll, in cirle on back. Courtesy Anita Pacey.

14'' Mary Hoyer. All hard plastic. This outfit is shown in the McCall's Needle Magazine of 1951. Courtesy Marge Meisinger. 14'' Composition -$75.00, 14'' Hard Plastic - $65.00.

HUMMEL

8'' All rubber Hummel boy. Pig goes in basket on back. Marks: M.J. Hummel - Bee Mark - /18-2, on head. Bee Mark/Ham 1800/W. Goebel/W. Germany, on back. 1966. Tag: Hummel Work. Courtesy Renie Culp. $85.00.

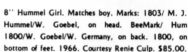

8'' Hummel Girl. Matches boy. Marks: 1803/ M. J. Hummel/W. Goebel, on head. BeeMark/ Hum 1800/W. Goebel/W. Germany, on back. 1800, on bottom of feet. 1966. Courtesy Renie Culp. $85.00.

12'' All vinyl. The arms, at shoulders, are very thin where they go into shoulders, not round but flat. Marks: Charlot Byj 2916, on head. W. Goebel 3906 (Bee Mark) W. Germany Gesch D.G.B.M. 1914035, on back. Tag: Hummel Werk. Courtesy Renie Culp. $20.00.

217

ICE CAPADES

All Ice Capade dolls are through the courtesy of Marlowe Cooper.

18" Ice Capades Skater. "Parisian Precision" 1958-1959. "Ice Capades, etc. label inside jacket hem. Each year the Ice Capades Costume Dept. costume dolls. (maker of dolls not important. This one happens to be an Alexander). By doing so they save a lot of money if errors show up before they make the real ones. The dolls are then used by Lighting and Screnery Depts. as models. A few of the earlier dolls have been sold to public. $300.00 up.

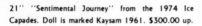

21" "Sentimental Journey" from the 1974 Ice Capades. Doll is marked Kaysam 1961. $300.00 up.

21" Kaysam 1961 doll that is called "Seasons" from the Ice Capades of 1973-1974. $300.00 up.

ICE CAPADES

24'' "Baby Doll Precision" Ice Capades 1970-1971. Doll is marked Kaysam 1961. $300.00 up.

24'' "American Girl" Ice Capades of 1970. Doll marked Kaysam 1961. $300.00 up.

1972 Ice Capades "The Legend of Frozen Times." Doll is marked Kaysam 1961. $300.00 up.

IDEAL

Shirley Temple: All composition, marked head or body, or both. First prices are for a mint and original doll. 2nd price is one with light craze, clouded eyes, and with original clothes. 3rd price is for cracked, badly crazed dolls not originally dressed.

11''	$175.00	$150.00	$ 85.00
13''	$130.00	$105.00	$ 65.00
16''	$145.00	$125.00	$ 75.00
18''	$165.00	$140.00	$ 85.00
22''	$200.00	$175.00	$ 95.00
25''	$300.00	$275.00	$100.00
27''	$450.00	$385.00	$125.00

Allow extra for special outfits, such as, the Cowgirl (Ranger), Wee Willie Winkie, Little Colonial, etc. $50.00-$100.00.

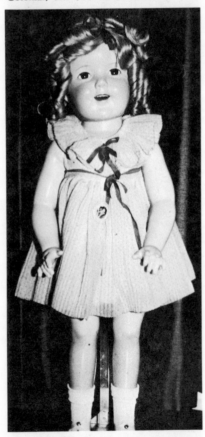

27''-28'' Shirley Temple. All composition and mint and original. Flirty eyes. Marks: Shirley Temple (curved)/Cop Ideal/No. 1. Courtesy Mary Sweeney. $450.00.

12'' Shirley Temple. All vinyl with sleep blue eyes and rooted saran hair. Original red dress with strips, bodice, lace edge of sleeves and purse with her name on it. 1957-58. Replaced shoes and sox. Courtesy Linda Crowsey. $45.00.

IDEAL

The following dolls are all Shirley Temple ''look-a-likes'' actually, they are copies of the Shirley Temple doll . . . some are very well made dolls and deserving to be added to a collection on their own merit. The majority of these look-a-likes will not be marked.

Imitation Shirley 16'' all original except sox. This doll was purchased from original owner. It was bought in 1935 by her godmother as a Shirley Temple. All composition - open mouth with 6 teeth. Hazel tin sleep eyes. No markings blonde mohair wig. Sue Austin Collection. $65.00.

221

IDEAL

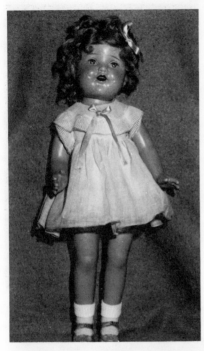

Imitation Shirley. All composition 25'' all original blue-green pleated organdy dress with pink trim pink shoes, open mouth for teeth - blue tin sleep eyes. Deep dimples. Marks: none. Blonde curly mohair wig. 1930. Sue Austin Collection. $110.00.

IDEAL

28'' Miss Charming. All composition and a very close Shirley Temple look-a-like. Blonde mohair wig set in Shirley like curls, brown/hazel or blue eyes. Open mouth. Copy of original clothes that look very much as a certain Shirley outfit. Made by owner. Marks: E.G., on head. Courtesy Sue Austin. 18'' - $180.00, 28'' -$275.00.

Shirley look-alike. All composition 19'' open mouth four teeth - green/grey eyes (sleep) - Blonde mohair -two dimples - wig. 1930's no markings. Sue Austin Collection. $85.00.

IDEAL

12" Fannie Brice. (Baby Snooks) Composition and wood with "flexie" wire arms and legs. Wood feet, composition hands. Hair molded with loop for ribbon bow. Painted blue eyes and open/closed mouth original yellow print outfit. Marks: Ideal Doll, on head. 1938. Courtesy Pearl Clasby. $165.00.

15" Judy Garland made and dressed for her role in The Wizard of Oz movie. All composition, large sleep brown eyes, open mouth. Marks: 15/Ideal Doll/Made in U.S.A., on head. Body: U.S.A./16. 1939. Courtesy Barbra Jean Male. Photo by Michael Male. $750.00.

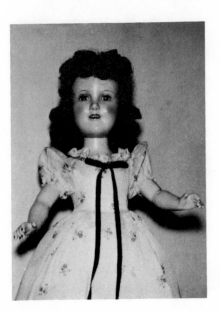

21" Judy Garland. All composition with glued on dark brown wig, sleep brown eyes and open mouth. Doll is marked with a backward "21". Gown is white with small flowers printed in and the ribbon is black. Courtesy Beth French. $165.00.

IDEAL

Ideal. Flossie Flirt 19''. All original, soft cloth body, composition head and legs, replaced rubber arms, flirty blue tin sleep eyes. Very detailed flapper-type mohair wig, white organdy dress with pink dots, white sox with pink stripes. 1934. Marks: none. Dimple in chin. Sue Austin Collection. $85.00.

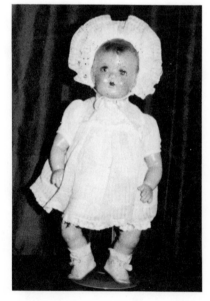

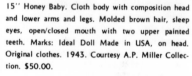

15'' Honey Baby. Cloth body with composition head and lower arms and legs. Molded brown hair, sleep eyes, open/closed mouth with two upper painted teeth. Marks: Ideal Doll Made in USA, on head. Original clothes. 1943. Courtesy A.P. Miller Collection. $50.00.

14'' Toni. All hard plastic with sleep eyes and nylon wig. All original. Open hands with index and little fingers extended above others. Marks: Ideal Doll/Made is U.S.A., on head. Ideal Doll/P-90, on back.1949. 14'' Toni - $40.00, 18'' Toni -$55.00, 21'' Toni - $70.00, 14'' Miss Curity -$60.00, 14'' Mary Hartine - $65.00.

IDEAL

21'' Toni. All hard plastic walker. All original and in original box. Red nylon wig. Marks: P-93/Ideal Doll. 14'' mint - $40.00, played with, dirty - $18.00. 18'' mint - $55.00, played with, dirty - $22.00. 21'' mint - $70.00, played with, dirty - $28.00.

16'' Baby Jo Anne. 1952. All stuffed warly vinyl jointed at shoulder, hips and neck. All fingers separate. Deeply molded hair, sleep blue eyes/lashes and lashes painted under eyes. Wide open/closed mouth with molded tongue. Marks: Ideal Doll, on head. Ideal Doll/16, on back. Matching boy (Billie) has molded hair and marked: B-23/Ideal Doll, on head. Courtesy Jayne Allen. $25.00.

23'' Posie. Hard plastic with vinyl head. Rooted brown hair, blue sleep eyes. Marks: Ideal Doll/VP-23 on head. Ideal Doll, Pat. Pending, on upper section of each leg. Jointed knees. Original Bride in trunk. 1954. Courtesy Penny Pendlebury. $35.00.

IDEAL

18'' Miss Revelon. All rigid vinyl with vinyl head. Rooted hair and sleep blue eyes. Pierced ears and jointed waist. Original dress of peach satin-taffeta. Matching short jacket. Marks: Ideal Doll/VT-18. 1955. Courtesy Ruth Fisher. 18'' - $45.00, 10½'' -$25.00.

30'' Baby Coo's. (Largest of the Baby Coo's line). Laytex one piece body and legs, disc jointed laytex arms. Hard plastic head with large sleep eyes, lamb's wool wig, open/closed mouth. All original. Made by Ideal. $85.00.

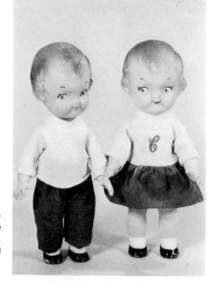

7½'' Campbell Kids of 1957. The 1955 set had cotton stuffed laytex bodies and limbs (one piece). These are all vinyl, jointed at necks, shoulders and hips. Painted features and molded hair. Outfits are red and white. Marks: Campbell Kids/Made by/Ideal Toy Co. Courtesy Kimport Dolls. $12.00 each.

IDEAL

42" Daddy's Girl. Plastic and vinyl with jointed waist and ankles. A very rare doll. Marks: Ideal Toy Corp/G-42-1/1960, on head. Shown below is a 38" Peter Playpal of 1960. Marks: Ideal Toy Corp./BE-35-38. Catalog reprint. $300.00, Peter -$165.00.

25" Bye Bye Baby. Vinyl and soft plastic body. Doll is strung. Blue sleep eyes, open mouth/nurser. Beautiful detailed. Marks: Ideal Toy Corp./L25NB, on head and body is not marked. Another just like this one is marked: Ideal Toy Corp./25N9, on head and Ideal Toy Corp. NB 25, on the back. Courtesy Phyllis Teague. $65.00.

29" Miss Ideal, the Photographer's Model. Plastic and vinyl with sleep eyes, closed smiling mouth and long rooted hair. Extra joints at waist, wrists and ankles. Original clothes. Marks: Ideal Toy Corp./SP-90-S, on head. 25" - $45.00, 29" - $65.00.

228

IDEAL

36'' Patti Playpal. Plastic and vinyl doll of 1961. All original. Marks: Ideal Doll/G-35, on head. Courtesy Jackie Shirley. $85.00.

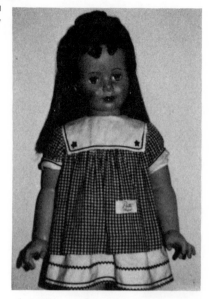

34'' Unusual Patti Playpal of 1961 in that she has straight, long red hair (rooted) and bangs. Plastic with vinyl head. Not original clothes. Marks: Ideal Doll/G-35. Courtesy Phyllis Teague. $85.00.

15 1/2 '' Carole Brent. Sold through Montgomery Wards in 1962. Painted eyes to side with modeled eyelids, all vinyl and original. Marks: Ideal Toy Corp/M-15-1, on head. Ideal Toy Corp/M-15, on back. This same doll was also used for Liz (1962) and mother of Tammy. $25.00.

IDEAL

22" Kissy of plastic and vinyl. Rooted hair and sleep eyes/lashes. Jointed wrists and open mouth. Press her arms together and she puckers and kisses. Marks: Ideal Toy Co./K-21-L, on head and Ideal Toy Co. Pat. Pend./4, on back. 1962. Courtesy Phyllis Teague. $25.00.

Ideal's Tammy is shown in one of the hardest to find outfits, that of a skier. The skis are excellent quality and have great detail and use metal springs. 1962. Skier - $15.00, Doll nude - $6.00.

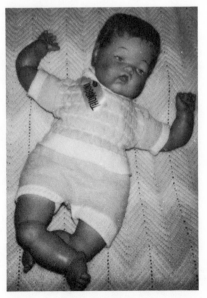

20" Thumbelina of 1967 and all original. Rooted hair, open/closed mouth, cloth body and vinyl head and limbs. Fingers and toes on one foot are curled. Marks; TT-18-H/Ideal Toy Corp. Courtesy Doris Richardson. $25.00.

IDEAL

9" Baby Betsy Wetsy. All vinyl with rooted hair, blue sleep eyes/molded lashes and long painted lashes at sides of eyes. Both index fingers extended. Open mouth/nurser. Marks: 1964/Ideal Toy Corp./B-W-9-4, on head. Ideal Toy Corp./1964/BW-9, on back. $12.00.

11½"-12" Super Heroines of 1967 made by Ideal. All vinyl with wired legs and arms that are posable. Eyes painted to the side. Marks: 1966/Ideal Toy Corp /W-12-3, on head. 1965/Ideal, in oval/T-12 with a 1 lower on hip. Tags: Ideal 1967, in oval/Japan. (Superwomen, others may vary slightly). Superdog is extremely rare. Catalog reprint. $35.00 each.

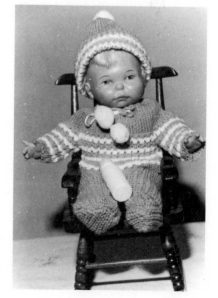

10½" Newborn Thumbelin. Cloth and vinyl with pull string in back that makes her squirm. Marks: 1967/Ideal, in circle, TT-8-H-108, on head. Painted eyes and closed mouth. Courtesy Phyllis Teague. $10.00.

231

IDEAL
IMPERIAL

17'' Baby Dreams. Foam filled body, peach covered top and white lower. Vinyl legs with all toes curled under on right foot. Rooted hair, sleep eyes/long lashes. ¾th arms and head are covered with ''peachy'' velour type material. Marks: 1974/Ideal and numbers that can't be made out, on head. Tag on clothes: Baby Dreams/1975 Ideal Hollis NY/Head made in USA/Doll body made in Hong Kong. $20.00.

20'' Mary Jo. All stuffed early vinyl. . the kind that turns orange. Sleep blue eyes/lashes. Disk jointed. Legs and body that of young girl. Rooted saran hair. All fingers separate and good detail. Marks: Imperial on head. 1950-1951. $30.00.

Bendables sold at Jack in the Box restaurants at Christmas Time. Names: Onion Ring Thing, Jack The Clown, Hamburger Meister, Small Fry and Secret Sauce Agent. Marks: Jack in the Box/Imperial/Hong Kong, with crown symbol. Courtesy Renie Culp. $40.00.

JUNEL
KAYSTAN

11'' All composition, painted eyes and glued on wig. Tag: Copy of Dress Worn By Julia Grant 1869/Junel Novelties, Inc. N.Y. The gown is peach satin. Courtesy Barbara McKeon. $22.00.

11'' All composition with painted eyes and glued on wig. Tag: Copy Of Dress Worn By Mary Lincoln 1861/Junel Novelties, Inc. N.Y. The gown is deep purple velvet with white sleeves and collar and gold trim. Courtesy Barbara McKeon. $22.00.

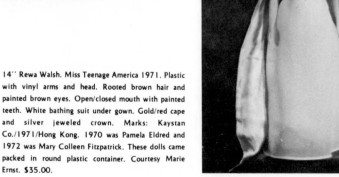

14'' Rewa Walsh. Miss Teenage America 1971. Plastic with vinyl arms and head. Rooted brown hair and painted brown eyes. Open/closed mouth with painted teeth. White bathing suit under gown. Gold/red cape and silver jeweled crown. Marks: Kaystan Co./1971/Hong Kong. 1970 was Pamela Eldred and 1972 was Mary Colleen Fitzpatrick. These dolls came packed in round plastic container. Courtesy Marie Ernst. $35.00.

KENNER

The most "desirable" of the Dusty outfits is the riding one. Her horse's name is "Nugget" and is velour covered with "hair" mane and tail. $10.00.

Dusty in her original golf outfit. Marked: G.M.P.G.I., on head. 1977 G.M.F.G.I. Kenner Prod./Made in Hong Kong, on back. $10.00.

Skye shown with the original Volleyball outfit and accessories. $10.00.

K & H
KRUSE, KATHE
LASTIC - PLASTIC

4'' Bisque quints with painted hair and eyes. Jointed shoulders and hips. Marks: K & H/U.S.A., on backs. Not original. Made by Kerr & Heinz of California. Courtesy Mary Williams. $12.00 each.

10'' Late Kathe Kruse girl with composition type (or mache) on cloth body. Courtesy Kimport Dolls. $100.00.

10½'' Our Girl. Stuffed vinyl with one piece body and limbs. Hand embedded long brown hair, blue sleep eyes, original clothes. Marks: Copyright 1952 Lastic Plastic, on back. Made by Fleischaker. Courtesy Margaret Mandel. $45.00.

LASTIC - PLASTIC
MAKER UNKNOWN

17'' Our Own Little Girl. All stuffed Lastic Plastic with flanged joints, wide spread legs, hand embedded blonde synthetic hair and blue eyes. Open mouth with tongue, no teeth. Replaced dress. Mark: Copyright 1951 Lastic Plastic. Courtesy Margaret Mandel. $45.00.

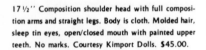

17 ½'' Composition shoulder head with full composition arms and straight legs. Body is cloth. Molded hair, sleep tin eyes, open/closed mouth with painted upper teeth. No marks. Courtesy Kimport Dolls. $45.00.

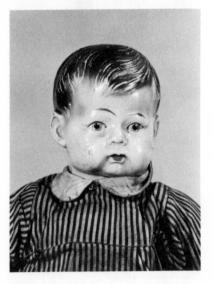

19'' Character boy with modeled hair, painted features and very full, low cheeks. Closed mouth. Tightly stuffed cloth body and limbs with composition lower arms. Wide spread legs, disc jointed and slightly bent. No marks. Courtesy Kimport Dolls. $65.00.

MAKER UNKNOWN

4'' (head only) Has a flange type neck, no marks and has a character face. Molded hair under wig, large painted eyes and impish smile. Head belongs to set called "FAMLEE" and came with 4 to 12 heads and one body. 1921. 4 head set: $175.00. Heads alone: $45.00. Courtesy Kimport Dolls.

3'' All bisque Quints with black molded, painted hair, painted eyes and one piece body and head. Made in Japan but not marked. Courtesy Phyllis Teague. $50.00 set.

17'' Mannequinn Doll that is painted plaster, well detailed painted features with molded hair. Original racoon coat. Most likely a furier's model. Unmarked. Ca. early 1930's. Courtesy Margaret Mandel. $42.00.

MAKER UNKNOWN

18'' Unknown composition with mohair wig braided and curly bangs. Hat and pinafore are original. She has an open mouth with felt tongue and 4 teeth. No marks. Courtesy Pam Ortman. $38.00.

Mfg. Unknown Girl, all composition, 15'' shiny yellow wig, closed mouth, blue plastic sleep eyes. Marks: none. Courtesy Austin Collection. $35.00.

13'' Unmarked composition. Slightly bent right arm. Brown tin eyes and original mohair wig. Redressed. Has all the appearance of an Alexander ''Betty'', but we can not be certain as neither the doll, nor the clothes are marked. Courtesy Margaret Mandel. $35.00.

MAKER UNKNOWN

3'' Baby that is all one piece molded rubber. Molded hair and wide open/closed mouth. Very good detail for such a small doll. Marks: none. Courtesy Pearl Clasby. $12.00.

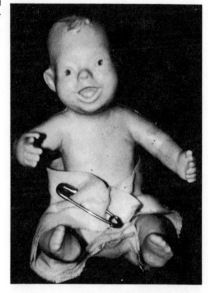

10'' Straw filled body with celluloid hands, shoes and head. Painted features. Marks: none. Courtesy Renie Culp. $9.00.

28'' All hard plastic walker. Head turns as she walks. Sleep blue eyes/lashes. Open mouth/teeth. Glued on wig. Eyeshadow. Original. No marks. $45.00.

MAKER UNKNOWN

23'' Majorette. All original hard plastic body vinyl head, blonde rooted hair closed mouth, blue plastic sleep eyes, dark blue felt costume with gold braid, white felt boots/gold tassles. Marks: none Mfg. unknown. Sue Austin Collection. $40.00.

18'' Wendy Girl, same construction as Billy-Boy. Navy jumper skirt with blue/white check top and red trim. Separate organza blouse with lace trim. She also came with a plaid dress with white pique insets in bodice and skirt. Courtesy Kimport Dolls. $38.00.

18'' Billy-Boy Bendee Doll. All bendable foam that has wired construction so they are completely posable. Sleep eyes and open/closed mouth. He is wearing light brown pants and green jacket with white shirt. He also came in blue jeans and plaid shirt. 1955. No marks. Courtesy Kimport Dolls. $42.00.

MAKER UNKNOWN

21'' Hard plastic head, sleep eyes/lashes. Closed mouth and molded hair. Very full cheeks and an unusual looking baby. Cloth body with vinyl arms and legs. Cryer in back. No marks. Courtesy Kimport Dolls. $40.00.

Nun. Mfg. unknown 19'' all original. All hard plastic open mouth four teeth, blue plastic sleep eyes. Marks: none. Sue Austin Collection. $35.00.

MAKER UNKNOWN

17" Miss America. (Marian McKnight - Miss South Carolina). 1957. Rigid vinyl with softer vinyl head. Rooted hair (originally had full bangs). Body and limbs have turned orange and head has remained pale. Sleep blue eyes/lashes with painted ones below eyes. Pierced ears and all fingers separate with 2nd and 3rd ones curled just slightly. High heel feet, deep red painted fingers and toes. Jointed waist. Original. White gown with imprinted (raised) white roses, silver on white lace trim. Blue ribbon: "Miss America" with stars dotting the i's. Plastic crown. Red velvet cape with white satin lining, fur trim and rhinestones. Originally the cape snapped (ties added). Silver plastic soled, cross strap shoes. $28.00.

36" Jodi Lynn is 1960 Aldens catalog, Honey Mate and Walking Wendy in 1961 catalogs. She came in several hair colors and lengths. Also was sold with baby buggy with attachment for her arm to rest in, and she walked along side buggy. Marks: AE/3561/25. Courtesy Phyllis Teague. $45.00.

242

MAKER UNKNOWN

25'' Dollspart's Co. doll (sold new for $5.00) Comes undressed. Rooted curly brown hair in vinyl head. Rest very light plastic. Open hands, sleep eyes and open mouth/nurser. Ca. 1960's. Courtesy Phyllis Teague. $25.00.

22'' Sun Maid Raisen doll. Dark brown rooted hair, brown sleep eyes. All original. Doll is unmarked. Ca. 1970's. Doll is plastic with vinyl head and arms. Courtesy Nancy Lucas. $28.00.

5½'' Joe-in li. All vinyl jointed at neck only. Molded clothes and ping pong paddle. Was to be used as centerpiece opposite Mr. Nixon at Republican Convention in San Diego. Convention site moved, so these table pieces were never used. $15.00.

1965 Color N Curl wig and head (added to body).
$30.00.

MATTEL

1962 Bubble cut Barbie with pale pink lips. $35.00.
(Also see Foreign Section.)

1963 Molded hair Barbie Fashion Queen. The blue
head band is removable (has molded hair band under
it). $30.00.

1964 Swirl bang Barbie. $15.00.

MATTEL

Herman Munster. Cloth and vinyl. Original. Tag: Herman Munster/1964 Kayre-Vue Productions/1964 Mattel Inc. Hawthorne California/USA/Pat'd in USA/Pad'd in Canada 1962/Other Patds. Pending. Courtesy Renie Culp. $18.00.

3'' Peter Paniddle shown with his ''dragon'', booklet and tiny Tinkerbell. The Tinkerbell is the same doll used as the tiny Barbie Doll. Made by Mattel in 1966. Courtesy Renie Culp. $10.00.

10'' Valerie. Plastic body with vinyl head and limbs. All original. Dress is marked Hong Kong and doll: 1967 Mattel Inc./U.S. & For./Pat. Pend./Hong Kong. Courtesy Renie Culp. $6.00.

MATTEL

11'' Small Talk Cinderella. Gown has lavender sleeves and deep rose inset with rest being gold thread thro gold colored material. Pull string talker. Marks: Japan, on head. 1967 Mattel Inc./U.S. & For./Pat. Pend/ Mexico, on back. Tag: Small Talk/1968 Mattel Inc./ Hong Kong. $10.00.

1968 Kiddle Kone. Stand is marked: 1966 Mattel Inc./Pat Pend. Hong Kong. Also: 1968 Mattel Inc./ Hong Kong. Doll is dressed in green and has greeen hair. Original. Courtesy Renie Culp. $5.00.

6½'' Pretty Pairs Lori (#1133). Came with Tiny Teddy Bear Tutti body of posable vinyl and all in one piece. Head looks like an over sized Kiddle. Dress has pink/blue flowers on white with pink cuffs & collar. The skirt is light blue/white stripes with deep rose colored rick-rack and lace. Panties are deep rose and dress is removable and snaps in the back. Had shoes and sox. No marks anywhere. 1969. Doll - $15.00, Set -$25.00.

MATTEL
MARX
MEGO

11½'' Barbie issued for the 1972 Montgomery Ward's 100th Anniversary. Doll came in brown mail order box or pink retail store box. Doll has curly bangs & ponytail, no red in nose, no color on toenails, no holes for earrings. She is tan toned color and has soft rubbery arms. Marks: Right hip: Midge TM/1962/Barbie/1958/by/Mattel, Inc./Patented. Head: 1968 Mattel/Inc. Japan. Right foot: Japan, across toes. Courtesy Renie Culp. $15.00.

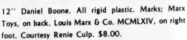

12'' Daniel Boone. All rigid plastic. Marks; Marx Toys, on back. Louis Marx & Co. MCMLXIV, on right foot. Courtesy Renie Culp. $8.00.

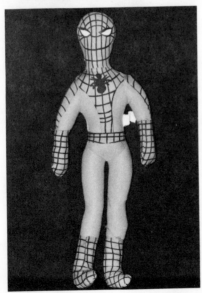

19'' Spiderman. All stuffed lithographed cloth and flannel. Eyes are pasted on. Tag: Mego Corp./Marvel Comics Group/Inc. 1974. This doll was made before the Spiderman became more popular with his own television series, and it may be re-introduced. $20.00.

248

MEGO

6'' Mickey from Our Gang. Same discription as others in this series. This is the doll that is hardest to find, as he was the one most wanted. Mickey grew up into Beretta/Robert Blake. Courtesy Marie Ernst. $15.00.

12'' Nubia of Wonderwomen. Uses the same body as Cher. Marked: Mego Corp. 1977/Made in Hong Kong, on back. Has rooted black hair with a white streak. Long inset lashes. Marked on head: D.C. Comics/Inc. 1976. $12.00.

MEGO

12'' Queen Hipplyte (Wonder-Women's mother) Uses the Cher body that is marked: Mego Corp. 1975/Made in Hong Kong on the lower torso. Blonde rooted hair, inset long lashes and green eyeshadow. Marked on head: 1976 D.C./Comics, Inc. $12.00.

12'' Steve Trevor of Wonderwomen. Full action figure and marked on the back: Mego Corp. 1977/Made in Hong Kong. Has brown molded hair and painted brown eyes. Open/closed mouth with painted teeth. Marked on head: 1976 D.C./Comics Inc. $12.00.

8'' Captain and Huggee-Bear from Starsky and Hutch series. Plastic and vinyl full action figures. By Mego and marked same as Starsky and Hutch. Captain -$8.00, Huggee Bear - $12.00.

MEGO
MILLER

18'' Million Dollar Baby. All vinyl with blue painted eyes, open/closed mouth and rooted hair. Excellent modeling and quality. Comes with silver plastic cup and spoon. Original. Fingers of right hand are curled to hold cup. Marks; 12/Mego Corp., on head. $30.00.

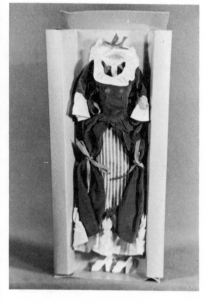

Cher outfit that seems to be very hard for collectors to find called Liberty Belle. 1977 and made by Mego. $10.00.

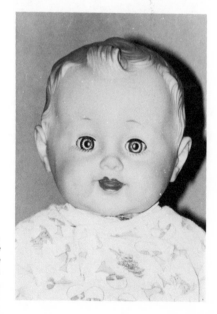

22'' All one piece stuffed laytex with early vinyl head. Deeply molded hair with large curl in front. Sleep blue eyes/lashes. Painted lashes under eyes. Wide open/closed mouth with modelled tongue. Cheek dimples. Deep red painted lips. Marks: MRP, on head. Made by Miller Rubber Co. $16.00.

MOLLYE

17" Kathryn Grayson. Kathryn was a very popular singer and actress. All composition with brown sleep eyes/lashes. Lightly touched black eyeshadow above the eyes. Closed mouth, pugged nose. Mohair wig. Not original clothes. Designed for Mollye. $85.00.

17" Profile view. She has an extremely pugged nose and protuding upper lip.

17" full length. The composition body looks very much like an Ideal body. Both hands are molded with all fingers together, except thumb, and slightly curled. The doll is completely unmarked.

NANCY ANN

All dolls are 5'' tall and are painted bisque. All are marked Nancy Ann Storybook on back. All courtesy Barbara McKeon. Bisque - $25.00, Hard Plastic - $12.00 to $16.00.

8'' Muffie. All hard plastic with sleep eyes and red mohair wig. Marks: Muffie/Storybook Dolls. There are unmarked Muffies. $25.00. Add extra for special outfits.

5'' Sunday's Child #186. Pale pink with darker pink trim and matching hat. $20.00.

5'' Monday's Child #180. White satin gown with blue net over-skirt and blue hat. $20.00.

5'' Tuesday's Child #181. Pink with pink trim and pale blue brows. $20.00.

NANCY ANN

5'' Wednesday's Child. #182. All in blues. Blue and pink flowers around base of skirt. $20.00.

5'' Thursday's Child #183. Yellow with red bows and trim. Red hat with yellow trim $20.00.

5'' Friday's Child #184. Pink with blue trim and blue/rose flowers on skirt. $20.00.

5'' Saturday's Child #185. Red skirt and hat. White figures and apron with red trim. $20.00.

5'' Spring. (No number). All pink with pink trim and pale blue ribbon on pink bonnet. $20.00.

5'' Summer. (No number). White with pink flowers, lavender bluish trim and bonnet. $20.00.

5'' Autumn. (No number). All deep violet. $20.00.

5'' Winter. (No number). Red dress, green jacket, green hat with green bow and red winter berry. $20.00.

6'' January #187-Merry Maid For New Year. Yellow skirt with orange and blue band, blue bodice and hat with yellow ribbon. $20.00.

6'' Febuary #188 Fairy Girl For Ice And Snow. All white with white net. $20.00.

6'' March-A Breezy Girl. #189. Pink with black trim and hat. $20.00.

6'' A Shower Girl For April. #190. Pink stripes and blue flowers on white gown. Pink trim around hat and pink umbrella. $20.00.

6'' A Rosebud Girl to Love Me Thru the June Days. #192. All pale pink with pale feather. $20.00.

6'' July-A Very Independent Lady for July # 193. Red with white stripes and blue hat and trim. $20.00.

6'' A Girl For August when it's warm. #194. Pink and pale blue, large flowers on pink gown. Pink ribbon and trim. $20.00.

6'' September Girl is Like a Storm. #195. Silver-grey with deep marroon panels and hat with matching grey ribbons. $20.00.

6'' A Sweet October Maiden Rather Shy. #196. All deep purple with lighter purple ribbons. $20.00.

6'' A November Lass to Cheer. #197. Beige skirt with brown trim and forest green bodice, pale yellow ribbon. $20.00.

6'' For December Just A Dear. #198. All red with white trim and furs-feathers. $20.00.

5'' Colonial Dame of the American Girl series - #56. Rose skirt with off white side panniers with blue and rose flowers. $20.00.

5'' Quakermaid #55 of American Girl Series. Silverish gray with white apron. $20.00.

5'' Western Miss #58 of the American Girl Series. Red/white checks with red apron with white trim. $20.00.

5'' Southern Belle #57 of American Girl Series. White with rose/red flowers and trim. Large black hat. $20.00.

5'' Curly Lock #154. Deep rose with white organdy apron with rose trim. Matching picture bonnet. $20.00.

5'' Left: Mary Had A Little Lamb #152. Pink with white figures, apron and hat. Right: Sugar and Spice #158. White with blue trim and hat. $20.00.

5'' There Was a Maiden Bright and Gay #175 (left). All pink with white and blue trim. Right: Jennie #161. Rose polka dot with white apron and trim. White bonnet. $20.00.

5'' Left: See Saw Majorie Daw #177. Pink flowers on pink gown, blue hat and feathers. Right: Princess Rosanie #162. All Pink. $20.00.

NANCY ANN

5'' Daffy Down Dilly #171. Pale yellow with bright yellow bodice, trim and hat. $20.00.

5'' Rain, Rain Go Away #170. Pink and blue flowers on white with blue cape and umbrella. Pink ribbon. $20.00.

5'' Daisy Belle #179. Yellow-gold with pink ribbon. $20.00.

5'' Silk and Satin #168. Dotted swiss with pale pink flowers, pale blue ribbon. $20.00.

5'' Beauty #156 - From Beauty and the Beast. All white with pale pink net. $20.00.

5'' Flossie #174. Green skirt, bodice and trim with white inset in skirt. Matching hat. $20.00.

5'' Little Miss Donnet, She Wore a Big Bonnet. #163. Large blue dots on white gown. Blue trim inside white bonnet. $20.00.

5'' Little Bo Peep #153. Pink/flowers. $20.00.

NANCY ANN

5'' Left: Nellie Bird, Nellie Bird #176. Lavender with deep purple on white with lavender trim apron. Carries straw broom. Right: Pretty Maid, Pretty Maid #160. White with blue ribbon and pink feather. $20.00.

Give Me A Lassie as Sweet as She is Fair. #178. Pale pink with deep purple bodice and bows. $200.00.

5'' Queen of Hearts #157. White with red bodice, red heart on skirt and bonnet. $20.00.

NANCY ANN
PLAYPAL

5'' Polly #173. Black gown, white apron with red bows. Cap is white with red bows. $20.00.

5'' Ring Around Rosy. #159. Rose gown with white trim and apron. Yellow blonde with white ribbon. $20.00.

5'' Nancy Ann Storybook and marked Japan. All bisque with painted features. ''Boots'' are white and painted on. Good quality clothes. Courtesy Diane Hoffman.

14'' Star Twinkle, Brenda Starr's baby. Plastic body with vinyl head and limbs. Bright red rooted hair over molded hair. Blue sleep eyes wih three painted lashes under the eyes. Open/mouth nurser. Marks: Playpal Plastic Inc./13 ME 1975, on head. $15.00.

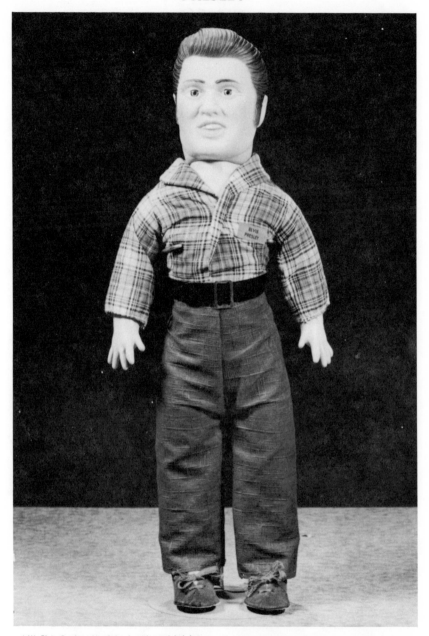

14'' Elvis Presley. Vinyl head with modeled hair, painted eyes and open/closed mouth with painted teeth. Magic skin (laytex) body. Marks: 1957 EPE or 1957 Elvis Presley Enterprises, on head. Original clothes. Courtesy Nancy Lucas. Mint - $450.00, Not original, but doll mint - $300.00, Laytex body bad, no clothes - $100.00.

REGENT
REMCO

5½'' Baby King, who is a "take-off" of Billie Jean King the tennis champion. All vinyl and jointed at neck only. Molded on clothes and painted on glasses. Marks: Regent Baby Products Corp./1973/Made in Korea. $4.00.

13¾'' Liza Littlechap. Plastic and vinyl with white streak in rooted hair. Blue eyeshadow. Marks: Liza/ Littlechap/Remco Industries/1963. Clothes will also be tagged with her name. Left leg is marked B92 and right leg B95. Courtesy Ruth Price. $25.00.

14½'' Dr. John Littlechap. Plastic and vinyl with molded hair and painted features. The doll is not marked, but any clothes will be tagged: Dr. John/Remco/Littlechap/Hong Kong. 1963. Courtesy Ruth Price. $25.00.

REMCO
ROBERTA

Remco went out of business in February of 1974, and the majority of their business was sold to Miner Industries. Miner has been marketing the ''Sweet April'' since then. The Miner Company has retained the ''Remco'' and are still using it.

15'' Orphan Annie. Plastic and vinyl with plastic disc eyes that move. Rooted red hair and no ears. Marks: Remco Ind. Inc./Copyright 1967. Courtesy Mary Williams. $25.00.

17'' Roberta Bride. All hard plastic, blonde mohair wig, blue sleep eyes, painted lashes below in original slipper satin gown trimmed in ecru cotton lace. Doll is unmarked. Made by the Roberta Doll Co. in 1946-47. Courtesy Margaret Mandel.

Close up of the Roberta Bride Doll. $32.00.

ROJAN
ROYAL
ROYALITY

7'' Little Boy Blue. All cloth with cotton clothes, yarn hair and painted features. Fastened with tab to box pictures of haystack. Box marked: Mother Goose Toys/ Rojan Toys/#503 Little Boy Blue. Courtesy Barbara Jean Male. Photo by Michael Male. $20.00.

19'' "Robin". She sold for $10.00 in 1966 at Marshall-Fields. Has same body construction as the "Lonely Liza" doll and a simular head, but different eyes. Cloth body with vinyl arms and legs. Vinyl head with rooted hair and large painted blue eyes to side. Pursed mouth. Wire runs through body for posing. Original red/white outfit. Marks: Royal Doll/1965, on head. $28.00.

8½'' Raggety Andy Doll Bank. Molded white clothes, painted black shoes, molded nose, set on black plastic eyes. Glued on yarn wig. Marks: Royalty, Ind. of Fla. Inc. 1974, on back of head and bottom of foot. Courtesy Penny Pendlebury. $18.00.

SAYCO
SEXED BABIES

10½" Miss America by Sayco. All vinyl with jointed waist. Sleep blue eyes. Marks: P, in circle, on head. Original. Also came with wardrobe. Courtesy Kimport Dolls. $20.00.

13" Sweet Nature Baby Tenderlove made by Mattel, Inc. Original panties only. One piece body and limbs. A sexed baby. Courtesy Phyllis Teague. $20.00.

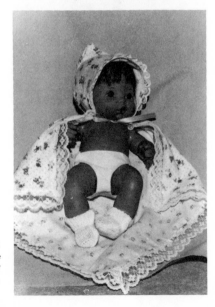

15" Tomasino by Furga of Italy. Open mouth/nurser, all vinyl, sleep eyes and sexed. Fully jointed, unlike most of the sexed babies. Original. Marks: Furga Italy/ 12401, on head and Furga Italy/10802, on back. Courtesy Phyllis Teague. $35.00.

269

SEXED BABIES

14'' Lil' David and Ruthie. Brother and sister sexed dolls. Original clothes. Body and limbs in one piece. Open mouth/nursers and painted eyes. Marks; Horsman 1976 on bodies. Courtesy Phyllis Teague. $20.00 each.

14'' David and Ruthie undressed. Courtesy Phyllis Teague.

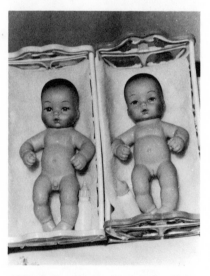

6'' Tiny Ruthie and Tiny David. All vinyl sexed dolls made by Horsman in 1978. Original clothes. Marks: Ruthie: 10, something unreadable-1978-6. David: B or 8-1978-6. $10.00 each.

6'' Tiny Ruthie and David undressed. Courtesy Phyllis Teague.

SEXED BABIES

11″ Adam and Eve Natural Babies. Sexed dolls by Eegee Doll Co. Original outfits, molded hair, open mouth/nursers, painted eyes and all vinyl. Courtesy Phyllis Teague. $18.00 each.

11″ Adam and Eve Natural Babies by Eegee undressed. Courtesy Phyllis Teague.

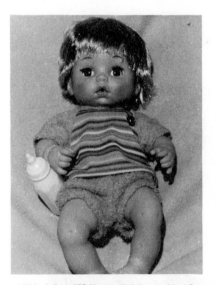

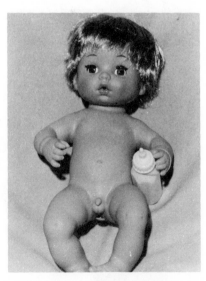

10″ Little Eric 1977 Playmate Doll Co. sexed boy. Excellent all vinyl with one piece body and limbs. Sleep eyes, open mouth/nurser and original clothes. Rooted hair. Marks: 17/20-8-76/8 110/Hong Kong, on head. 24/8110 Playmate/Hong Kong 20-8-76, on back. Courtesy Phyllis Teague. $16.00.

10″ Little Eric undressed. Courtesy Phyllis Teague.

SHINDANA
SUN RUBBER
TERRI LEE

15½'' Marla Gibbs. Plays the maid on the T.V. series, "The Jeffersons." Also is packaged with a ball gown. All plastic with vinyl head and rooted hair. Painted brown eyes, open/closed mouth with painted teeth. Marks: 1978/Shindana Toys/Hong Kong, on head. Hong Kong, on back. $20.00.

17'' Bannister Baby. Early Lastic-Plastic vinyl that turns dark. Molded hair, sleep eyes and open mouth/nurser. Marks: Constance Bannister (famous baby photographer) New York, New York, on head. Mfg. by Sun Rubber Co. Courtesy Phyllis Teague. $40.00.

This is a group of Terri Lee, Jerri Lee dolls (back row) and a Tiny Terri Lee in check coat, plus the regular Linda Baby and the missing, Linda Lee. Her clothes are tagged: Linda Lee. All vinyl with painted features.

Courtesy Judy Perez. 16'' Terri Lee - $75.00, 16'' Terri Lee - $95.00, 10'' Tiny Terri Lee - $60.00, 10'' Linda Baby - $85.00, 14'' Linda Lee - $100.00.

TERRI LEE

16" Terri Lee. Left one is all composition and wears a tagged black and white checked coat and sandals made for Ideal's Giggles doll. Right Terri Lee is all rigid vinyl and wears tagged cowgirl outfit. The shirt was used on the Jerri Lee doll. Courtesy Florence Black Musich. Compo - $95.00, Hard Plastic - $75.00.

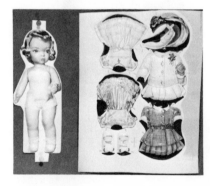

9" Tall Terri Lee and her clothes. Three-D molded plastic. Made after plant was moved to Apple Valley, California. $30.00 complete set.

Some of the additional pieces of clothing for the Terri Lee Paperdoll.

TERRI LEE
TROLLS

16'' Terri Lee Eskimo. Dark skin tones with black wig. Doll is rigid vinyl. Original tagged Eskimo suit with red pants and white fur. Doll is marked: Patent Pending. Courtesy Shirley Smith. $120.00.

16'' Terri Lee in Brownie Uniform. Plastic with painted features. Marks: Terri Lee/Pat. Pending, on back. Courtesy Mary Sweeney. $80.00.

12'' Trolls that are marked: Dam Things 1964, on feet. Girl has deep rose hair and ''jumper'' with yellow top. He has yellow hair and top with blue pants. Courtesy Renie Culp. 3''-4'' - $4.00-$7.00, 7'' -$12.00, 12'' - $18.00.

TROLLS

12'' Girl: Cloth body with cloth tag: Ideal. Vinyl arms and head. Head is incised: Scandia House Enterprises. 12'' Boy: Cloth body with no tag, legs are in corduroy (girl has felt legs). Vinyl head and arms. Head is incised: Scanda House Enterprises. There are very rare Trolls. Courtesy June Schultz. $18.00.

11'' Viking Troll marked: Thomas Dam. Tan felt suit, holds sword and has heavy beard as well has hair and horns are molded to hat. All trolls have fur hair, but Uneeda made some with mohair during 1973. (These sold for $1.25) Courtesy June Schultz. $16.00.

The Troll animals are highly collectable and rather scarce. This one is a monkey that is all vinyl and jointed at the neck. 7½'' tall and marked: R Shekter 1966, on one foot and U.S.A., on other foot. Arms are molded so it can hold onto things. Courtesy June Schultz. $20.00 each.

UNEEDA
VOGUE

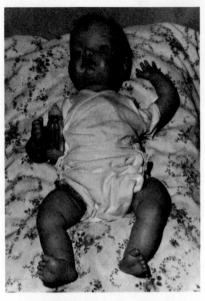

19" Wiggles made by Uneeda Doll Co. Has oil cloth outer body covering with vinyl limbs attached. Vinyl body and head. Inset eyes, rooted hair, open mouth/nurser and has cryer. Marks: Uneeda Doll/NF21, on head. Courtesy Phyllis Teague. $50.00.

Vogue's Jill and Jeff. All hard plastic Jill and Jeff is plastic and vinyl. Both have sleep eyes. Both are shown in there original ski outfits. Jill - $30.00, Jeff -$35.00.

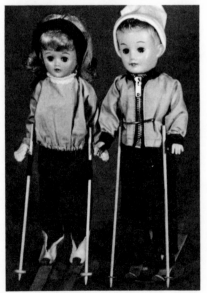

10" Suzette & 11" Bob. King Arthur and Queen Guinivere. He: Black body suit & boots. Gold vest, black plastic belt and red cape & hat. She: Gold bodice with white skirt. Both are marked Uneeda on head and back. Courtesy Marie Ernst. She - $12.00, He -$14.00.

VOGUE

Toodles. All composition. 7''-8''. Painted eyes to side. Mint and original - $75.00. Special outfits - to $100.00. Light craze, played with, original - $45.00. Special outfits -to $60.00. Craze, not original - $25.00.

Toodles baby. Mint and original - $65.00. Light craze, played with, original -$45.00. Craze, not original clothes - $20.00.

Hard plastic Ginny with painted eyes. Mint and original - $65.00. Played with, original - $45.00. Not original clothes - $20.00.

Hard plastic Ginny. Straight leg, non walker. Mint and original - $50.00. Special outfits - to $100.00. Played with, original - $35.00. Special outfits -to $60.00. Not original clothes - $20.00.

Straight leg, walker Ginny. Mint and original - $45.00. Special outfits - to $75.00. Played with, original - $30.00. Special outfits -to $60.00. Not original clothes - $18.00.

Bend knee Ginny. Mint and original - $40.00. Special outfits - to $65.00. Played with, original - $25.00. Special outfits -to $45.00. Not original clothes - $15.00.

Lamb's wool wig Ginny. Mint and original - $65.00. Played with, original - $45.00. Not original clothes - $20.00.

Bent leg Ginny Baby. Mint and original - $65.00. Not original clothes - $45.00.

7 ½'' Toodles (Ginny) by Vogue. All composition and all original as a fireman. Painted eyes to side and glued on mohair wig. Also in this series were: policeman, mailman, nurse, solider, sailor, marine, aviator and yachting captain. Doll - $75.00. In this outfit -$100.00.

VOGUE

7½" Toodles (Ginny). All composition with bent right arm, painted features with eyes to the side. Original Indian outfits and in original boxes. Courtesy Barbara Boury. Dolls - $75.00 each. In this outfits -$100.00 each.

8" Ginny. One of the first in hard plastic with sleep eyes. Lamb's wool wig, no lashes and straight leg, non-walker. All original. $65.00.

Vogue's Wee Imp. All hard plastic with orange hair and freckles. The sleep eyes are green. This outfit is tagged Vogue Dolls. #6150-1956. $65.00.

VOGUE

8'' Ginny in cowboy and cowgirl outfits. The outfits are black with silver trim and they wear white scarfs. Both dolls and clothes are tagged and marked. Courtesy Barbara Boury. Dolls - $50.00. In this outfit - $100.00.

8'' Ginny with tag: Linda/No. 21. Other side: A Vogue Doll. Black pupiless sleep eyes with painted lashes over eyes. Velvet flowers in hair. Dress in pink organdy embossed with white flowers and squares with lace at hem and sleeves. Pink trim/ribbon. Matching panties and pink shoes and socks. Straight leg, non-walker. Courtesy Marjorie Uhl. $50.00.

8'' Ginny. All hard plastic. Straight leg, walker. All original. Marks: Ginny/Vogue Dolls Inc. Red velvet, plaid taffeta skirt and black velvet trim. Courtesy Barbra Jean Male. $45.00.

VOGUE

14" Ginny. Plastic and vinyl. Date unknown. In a beautiful blue and black gown with matching hat and purse. Courtesy Mary Williams. $25.00.

14" Ginny Nun. Plastic and vinyl with sleep eyes, all original. Date unknown. Marks: Vogue Doll, on head. Courtesy Mary Williams. $25.00.

15" My Angeline. All vinyl with sleep blue eyes/lashes. Light pink fingernail polish. Freckles. Original plaid dress. Marks: Doll, on head. Vogue Doll/1965, on body. Tag: Vogue Dolls Inc. Head designed by Deet and body by Italian sculpter Ungars. Courtesy Burnie Freeman. $20.00.

VOGUE

12'' Musical Baby Dear. Cloth and vinyl with painted features and rooted hair. Music box in back, key wound. Marks: Vogue Dolls, Inc. and E. Wilkins/ 1960, on upper leg. Courtesy Doris Richardson. $22.00.

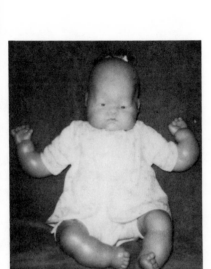

17'' Baby Dear. All original with top knot of rooted hair. Painted features. Cloth body with vinyl head and limbs. Marks: Vogue Dolls, Inc., on head. E. Wilkins/ 1960, on upper leg. Courtesy Doris Richardson. Top Knot - $40.00. Bald head - $35.00.

17'' Too Dear. Very fat toddler and all vinyl with rooted hair and sleep eyes. Marks: 1963 Eloise Wilkin. The designer of the doll was Eloise Wilkins and she was made by Vogue Co. Courtesy Phyllis Teague. $85.00.

VOGUE

17'' Too Dear by Vogue Dolls. Same description as one on preceeding page, except this example is all original. Courtesy Doris Richardson. $85.00.

8½'' Miss Ginny. All vinyl. Am sure this is wrong body as head is too big. Sleep blue eyes/molded lashes. Open/closed mouth with two molded teeth. Long rooted hair. Marks: Vogue Doll/1967, on head. $10.00.

18'' Baby Dear of 1967. Cloth with vinyl head and limbs. Sleep eyes, closed mouth and rooted hair. Also was made with molded hair. Marks: Vogue Doll 1965, on head. Courtesy Phyllis Teague. $25.00.

NUMBER INDEX

LETTERS & SYMBOLS

<table>
<tr><td></td><td>- 89</td><td></td><td>- 20</td></tr>
<tr><td></td><td>- 57</td><td></td><td>- 130</td></tr>
<tr><td></td><td>- 57</td><td></td><td>- 17</td></tr>
<tr><td></td><td>- 58</td><td></td><td>- 15</td></tr>
<tr><td></td><td>- 83</td><td></td><td>- 26</td></tr>
<tr><td></td><td>- 81</td><td></td><td>- 17</td></tr>
<tr><td></td><td>- 89</td><td></td><td>- 49</td></tr>
<tr><td></td><td>- 131</td><td></td><td>- 14</td></tr>
<tr><td></td><td>- 76, 217</td><td></td><td>- 23</td></tr>
<tr><td></td><td>- 81</td><td></td><td>- 10</td></tr>
</table>

HEU BACH - 84, 85

- 84

G - 47, 84

IDEAL - 90

K R - 73, 94-96

K.W. G. - 105